Lecture Notes in Artificial Intelligence 11957

Subseries of Lecture Notes in Computer Science

More information about this series at http://www.springer.com/series/1244

Tobias Ahlbrecht · Jürgen Dix ·
Niklas Fiekas (Eds.)

The Multi-Agent Programming Contest 2018

Agents Teaming Up in an Urban Environment

 Springer

Editors
Tobias Ahlbrecht ⓘ
TU Clausthal
Clausthal-Zellerfeld, Germany

Jürgen Dix ⓘ
TU Clausthal
Clausthal-Zellerfeld, Germany

Niklas Fiekas ⓘ
TU Clausthal
Clausthal-Zellerfeld, Germany

ISSN 0302-9743 ISSN 1611-3349 (electronic)
Lecture Notes in Artificial Intelligence
ISBN 978-3-030-37958-2 ISBN 978-3-030-37959-9 (eBook)
https://doi.org/10.1007/978-3-030-37959-9

LNCS Sublibrary: SL7 – Artificial Intelligence

Preface

In this volume, we present the 13th edition of the annual Multi-Agent Programming Contest and its participants.

The 2018 scenario and all its changes from previous competitions are described in the first contribution, together with a brief description and analysis of the five participating teams and a closer look at the matches. This is followed by a contribution from each team, where they introduce the methods and tools they employed to create their agent team and where they analyze their performance and the contest from their point of view.

A single-blind review has been conducted for each paper by at least two reviewers. Each team was able to pass the review process successfully.

October 2019

Tobias Ahlbrecht
Jürgen Dix
Niklas Fiekas

Organization

Program Chairs

Jürgen Dix   TU Clausthal, Germany
Tobias Ahlbrecht   TU Clausthal, Germany
Mehdi Dastani   Utrecht University, The Netherlands
Niklas Fiekas   TU Clausthal, Germany

Program Committee

Federico Schlesinger   Zalando, Germany
Evangelos Sarmas   .
Alessandro Ricci   University of Bologna - Cesena Campus, Italy
Sebastian Sardina   RMIT, Australia
Peter Novak   Meandair, The Netherlands

Contents

The Contest

The Multi-Agent Programming Contest 2018 - A Third Time in the City

Tobias Ahlbrecht$^{(\boxtimes)}$ ⓘ, Jürgen Dix ⓘ, and Niklas Fiekas ⓘ

Department of Informatics, Clausthal University of Technology,
Clausthal-Zellerfeld, Germany
{tobias.ahlbrecht,dix,niklas.fiekas}@tu-clausthal.de
http://cig.in.tu-clausthal.de

Abstract. We present the thirteenth edition of the annual Multi-Agent Programming Contest, a community-serving competition that attracts participants from all over the world. Participants have to design a program that controls entities in a specifically designed scenario. This challenge is interesting in itself and also well-suited to be used in educational environments. Usage of multi-agent technology is encouraged and allows for comparison of different multi-agent systems and also conventional approaches. This time, five teams competed using strictly agent-based as well as traditional programming approaches.

Keywords: Multi-agent systems · Programming · Competition

1   Introduction

In this introductory article, we (1) briefly elaborate the motivation behind our Contest[1] and its 13-year history, (2) explain the current scenario and how it evolved to its third iteration, (3) introduce the five teams that took part this time, (4) analyze key matches to draw conclusions about the participants, the current scenario, and the contest as a whole, and (5) evaluate each team's performance from our point of view.

The Multi-Agent Programming Contest (MAPC) has been organised (almost) annually since 2005. It was established by Jürgen Dix and Mehdi Dastani with a lot of help from Peter Novák, who fully joined the effort later. The competition was held in 2018 for the 13th time.

The goal of the Contest is to encourage and support research in the field of multi-agent system engineering by (1) identifying key problems and challenges, (2) developing suitable benchmarks, (3) comparing agent programming languages and platforms, and (4) compiling test cases which require and enforce

---

[1] https://multiagentcontest.org.

The original version of this chapter was revised: In chapter 3.3 the paragraph on TUBDAI's work was revised. The correction to this chapter is available at https://doi.org/10.1007/978-3-030-37959-9_7

T. Ahlbrecht et al. (Eds.): MAPC 2018, LNAI 11957, pp. 3–22, 2019.
https://doi.org/10.1007/978-3-030-37959-9_1

coordinated action that can serve as milestones for testing multi-agent programming languages, platforms and tools. Moreover, we aim to support educational efforts in the design and implementation of multi-agent systems: our scenario is ready to use and provides a concrete problem for agent systems to solve.

The scenario is basically a game that an autonomous program has to play. The state of the environment is handled by our server, to which each agent is connected remotely. At the beginning of each simulation step, the current environment state is sent to each agent. Then, the agents have 4 s to reason about it and decide which action to execute next. The server gathers all actions and executes them to generate the next environment state. This process is repeated for a predefined number of steps.

1.1   Related Work

For a detailed account on the history of the contest as well as the underlying simulation platform and previous iterations of the contest, we refer to [1,4,5,7–10,13,14,21], especially the contests of 2016 [2] and 2017 [3], which were using the same base scenario as the current contest. A quick non-technical overview appeared in [6].

While there have been many contests organized in the last decade, targetting agent systems or AI in general, there is no other competition with the same focus as the Multi-Agent Programming Contest.

Starting in 2001, the *Trading Agent Competition* [25] was held, featuring a market game for agents to play. From 2003, it featured a supply-chain management scenario until 2009. In 2012, it was superseded by the *Power Trading Agent Competition* [20], which specializes on agents trading in the energy market. It is overall more focussed on the performance of single agents and good strategies.

Another competition using agents is the well-known *Agent Simulation* part of the *RoboCup Rescue Simulation League*, where agents have to work in the aftermath of an earthquake. Participants have to use the competition's *Agent Development Framework*.

There are also a number of *Planning Competitions*[2], e.g. the *RoboCup Logistics League*[3], which address the planning aspect of multi-agent systems.

And of course, there are a lot of competitions based on even more game-lie scenarios. Some require the autonomous program to deal with existing games, like the *Student StarCraft AI tournament*[4] or the *Mario AI Championship* [19], and some use games which are purpose-built for each competition, like *BattleCode*[5]. The difficulty in most of these games of course lies in the "real time" aspect. Additionally, the interesting part is whether the program can play the game as well or even better as a human player. In the case of *BattleCode* on the other hand, other restrictions are placed on the agents, like e.g. the amount of communication or the number of byte-code instructions that can be executed.

---

[2] http://ipc.icaps-conference.org/.
[3] http://www.robocup-logistics.org/sim-comp.
[4] http://sscaitournament.com/.
[5] https://www.battlecode.org.

To conclude, our Contest has a number of notable distinctions.

– We do not require a specific programming language or approach.
– We do not focus on solutions or good strategies for a particular problem domain.
– We focus on desirable qualities of multi-agent systems, like communication and cooperation.

2   MAPC 2016 to 2018: Evolution of the City Scenario

In the "City scenario"[6], agents have to traverse realistic street graphs of different cities and complete random assignments. These assignments reward currency, which has to be spent to build (water) wells, which will generate score points for the building team until they are dismantled.

An example of the visualization is given in Fig. 1. Agents are represented as vehicle symbols while facilities are depicted as pins. Facilities are fixed locations on the map where agents can perform specific actions.

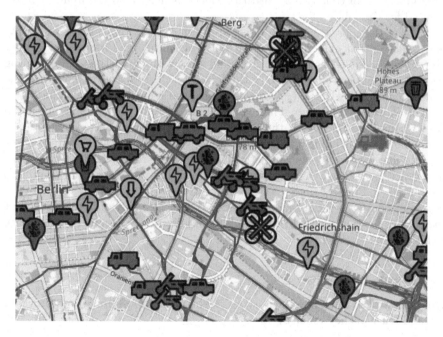

Fig. 1. Visualisation of the City scenario © OpenStreetMap (www.openstreetmap.org/copyright)

---

[6] The complete documentation can be found at https://github.com/agentcontest/massim/tree/858fb9f75ae5d4036cc6a9ffe439f4052d0414ff/docs.

2.1 Items

An item is characterised by its name, volume and associated value. The most basic items (also called resources) can be obtained for free at *resource nodes*. Then, there are a number of items that can only be gained by assembling them from other items. These *assembled items* require (i) the agents performing the assembling process to carry at least certain amounts of specific items, and (ii) particular agent roles to participate in the assembling.

All items together can be viewed as an *item graph*, where each item type is a node and a directed edge between two items means that one is required to assemble the other.

2.2 Jobs

To earn currency, an agent team has to buy *items* from *shops* and coordinate to assemble these to more complex items. Those assembled items then have to be delivered to specific *storage* locations to complete a *job*. That is, a job describes a set of items that have to be delivered to a particular location. Jobs also have a deadline and, of course, a reward that depends mostly on the items that are required for the job.

Most of the jobs, the *regular* jobs, are posted for both agent teams at the same time, so that only the team that delivers the required items first will get the reward. *auction jobs* on the other hand start with an auction phase. During this time, agents can place bids for the job. In each step, both teams learn the current lowest bid. At the end of this phase, the team that placed the *lowest* bid will be awarded the job. The team will also only receive the amount it bid once it completes the job. If the team then does not manage to complete the job within the time limit, it has to pay a fine. While auction jobs are rather less valuable due to both teams competing for the lowest reward, it is more safe as the team it is assigned to does not have to fear that the other team completes the job faster. Finally, *missions* were introduced to compare teams working on the same job at the same time. A mission is basically like an auction job, but without the auction phase, so that each team is instantly assigned one instance of this job.

2.3 Agents and Roles

Agents control 4 different vehicle types in the simulation: drones, motorcycles, cars and trucks. They differ by

- speed (how many "units" they can travel in one step),
- vision (how far the agent can "see", in meters),
- load (how much they can carry), and
- battery (how often they can move before they have to recharge).

Additionally, drones are the only agents that can fly. All other agents are bound to the street graph. The current values for each role's attributes are summarised in Table 1. If two values are given, the first one is the start value while the second one describes the maximum value for that attribute. This is due to the *upgrade system*, that allows agents to spend their rewards to improve themselves rather than build facilities that increase their score.

Table 1. Agent roles

Name	Agents	Speed	Vision	Load	Battery	Skill
Drone	4	5/7	600/1000	15/25	20/40	1/3
Motorcycle	8	4/6	500/900	30/70	30/60	6/10
Car	10	3/5	400/800	50/150	40/80	8/12
Truck	12	2/3	300/700	100/300	50/100	10/15

We see that there are only 4 drone agents, while the number of agents increases, as their speed and vision decrease, while load, battery and skill increase. In the 2018 Contest, items were configured to have a random volume between 5 and 10. Thus, drones could carry between 2 and 5 items, while trucks could handle many more.

2.4 Percepts

Percepts are sent as XML messages to each agent at the beginning of each step, encoding the current world state. When a simulation starts or an agent first connects into a running simulation, general information about that simulation is perceived, like the characteristics of the agent's role, the items that exist in the simulation (and possibly how to assemble them), the upgrades that can be bought and their costs and the types of wells that can be built (see Sect. 2.5).

The perceptions that are sent each turn include an agent's location, current battery charge or how much load capacity is used. Agents also learn about the result of their last action and which items they are currently carrying. In addition, the location of other agents and the current state of all (visible) facilities is transmitted. Finally, each agent receives a list of all jobs that are currently active.

2.5 Actions and Facilities

After an agent has received percepts, the server expects an answer including the agent's next action within 4 s. The server gathers all actions and processes them in random order, updating the world state, before the next step begins. Facilities are mostly fixed locations on the map, where agents can or have to perform different actions to reach their goals. Agents can choose from the following set of actions.

goto: Allows an agent to move to a specified location. If the location cannot be reached by the agent in one step due to its distance, the internal routing algorithm is used to determine a complete route to the location and the agent moves to the first point of that route (i.e. as far as its speed allows). Locations can be the names of facilities or raw coordinates. Using this action consumes exactly 1 energy point.

charge: This action can only be used at `charging stations` to charge the agent's battery back up.

recharge: This action also restores some charge of the agent. It can be used everywhere, but is way less effective than charging at a `charging station`. It is intended to be used when an agent failed consider visiting `charging station` in its plan. Only 1 battery point is restored and only if the action is successful, which is only in about 30% of attempts.

give/receive: Two agents can use this pair of actions to transfer items among them. Both agents have to be in the same[7] location.

store/retrieve: These actions can be used at `storage` facilities, to temporarily store items.

assemble: This action is used to initiate the assembling process. The agent using this action has to specify the item that is to be created. Additionally, all assembling agents have to be at a `workshop` facility.

assist_assemble: All agents who want to help one agent assemble an item have to use this action and specify the agent they want to assist. All of these agents have to be at the same location. The assembling process then takes all required items from the agents and gives the requested item to the agent that initiated the process.

deliver_job: This is the action to deliver items towards completion of a job. The agent has to specify the particular job and be at the correct `storage` for that job. The action automatically deposits all items of that agent that are still missing for the job.

bid_for_job: To bid for an auction job, agents can use this action. It requires the job and the amount of currency (i.e. the reward) that should be bid.

dump: This action can be used at `dump` facilities to destroy items.

gather: Gathering at `resource nodes` is the only way to acquire base items. An internal counter in each node determines after how many actions an item is given out, so that using multiple agents for gathering is more effective. Also, both teams gathering at the same time at the same node will manipulate the same counter, while only the lucky agent putting it over the threshold will actually get the item. To make it more challenging and encourage exploration of the map, resource nodes are only visible if an agent is in close proximity.

build/dismantle: The `wells` can be created and removed with these actions. Agents have to get rewards from completing jobs and use them as a resource to build wells. Wells can be built at any location where no other facility exists yet. They start off with a base *integrity* level after one agent has used

---

[7] To be in the same location in this scenario is defined as sharing the same coordinates up to the x-th digit after the decimal place.

the `build` action. Further `build` actions are then required to finish the well. A finished well will generate a certain amount of score points per step for as long as it exists. As resource nodes, wells are also hidden (from the opposing team) until an agent is in close proximity, since agents can also use the `dismantle` action to reduce a well's integrity until it reaches 0 and the well finally vanishes. We introduced wells mainly to increase interaction between the teams.

trade: Items can also be sold at `shops` using this action. This is only a way to avoid completing jobs in the beginning, as `shop` prices are intentionally kept unfavourable.

2.6 Winning

As mentioned above, the agents' goal for the 2018 contest was split into two tiers. On the one hand, agents had to earn resources from completing jobs by gathering and assembling items. On the other hand, the agents had to make use of these resources and build and defend wells to accumulate *score* points. The team with the highest score wins the game and earns three tournament points. In case of a draw, both teams would have earned 1 point (though this did not occur).

2.7 Evolution of the Scenario

The same base scenario was already played in 2016 and 2017, from where it slowly evolved to its current form.

Starting in 2016, the main goal was to earn as many rewards as possible from completing jobs. The well mechanic was only added in 2017 to increase interaction between the teams and make the current state of the simulation more visible. Due to the newly added wells, the *skill* attribute was introduced, determining the efficiency of `build`, `dismantle` and also `gather` actions, with drones being least efficient and generally giving a role higher skill the slower it is. Drones got an especially low skill value as they can build wells all over the map. Also, the upgrade system was newly introduced for the 2018 Contest.

The availability of items also changed each year. In the first City scenario, all items (even assembled ones) could be bought in shops, while assembling them from other items was much cheaper. Unfortunately, all teams just opted for the easy solution of buying all items, which meant that no team benefitted from the assembling feature. Thus, in the next Contest, only base items/resources could still be bought in shops to force teams to use the *cooperative* assembling mechanic. Resource nodes were also established in the second iteration of the contest as an alternative to buying base items from shops. As we had seen many idle agents in the previous year, this change would reward more *proactive* agents. In the latest scenario instance, resource nodes have then become the only way to get base items at all, since different shop prices did not prove to be an interesting factor anymore. Also, having two different goal components - the jobs and wells - meant we had to streamline the scenario where possible. For 2016 and 2017, items required specific tools to be assembled and each tool could only be used by a specific agent role. For 2018, tools were removed and items now require specific agent roles to be present in the assembling process. This was again changed to simplify the overall process.

Only in 2017, charging stations could be subject to a blackout, which effectively disabled them for a number of steps. Since this did not generate a notable impact, this feature was removed again in 2018.

A traditional change in the Contest is always to increase the number of agents for each new iteration. We started with 16 agents (4 of each type) in 2016 and continued with 28 agents (4 more per role, except for drones) in 2017. In 2018, another 6 agents were added (2 cars and 4 trucks), totaling 34 agents.

3   The Tournament

The 2018 Contest took place on September 24th and 25th, after a short qualification phase where all five teams had to demonstrate that they could reliably receive messages from and send messages to one of our servers. Fortunately, no team got disqualified. In the tournament, each team had to face off against each other team in a match consisting of three simulations each.

3.1   Simulation Setup

Each match between two teams consisted of three separate simulations. We used again three different sets of parameters to configure these simulations, so that the teams had to compete in three different settings. A simulation consisted of 1000 steps. Each team started with 5000 massium, so that one or two wells could be immediately built.

The first simulation was always played on a street map of (a part of) Copenhagen. The *item graph* contained 5 base items that could be assembled to more complex items (which could be required themselves for even more complex items). With a chance of 30%, a new job was generated in each step. 5% of these jobs were auctions and only 0.03% were missions (since the focus should shift to the wells and their placement). These first simulations also provided the jobs with the smallest rewards out of all three types of simulations. Facility parameters were set up identically for all simulations. Resource nodes were configured to be the second most common of facilities, so as to diminish the effect of luck in finding specific nodes. Charging stations were actually the most common type of facility. They should be considered by the agents, without being overly restrictive on their possible routes. All simulations were configured to generate two available types of wells. One that generated 1 score point per step, and one that generated 2 points, but was more expensive upfront.

In the second simulation, played on a map of Berlin, rewards were increased slightly, so that more wells could be built. In addition, the item graph only contained 4 base items, reducing the complexity of completing jobs. The area of the map was bigger than in the first simulation. All in all, completing jobs should have been easier, while locating wells of the opposing team might have become more challenging.

We continued the trend with the third simulation, played on a map of São Paulo[8]. The area that was played on was again larger than before. The item graph was reduced to 3 base items and the rewards were significantly increased, so that most jobs allowed a team to build multiple wells at once.

3.2   Participants and Results

Five teams participated in the Multi-Agent Programming Contest 2018, as listed in Table 2 in alphabetical order. All of the teams had an academic background. Two came from Brazil, another two from Germany and one from Denmark. Besides, each team had at least one member (or supervisor) who had taken part in at least one previous Contest.

Table 2. Participants of the 2018 Contest.

Team	Affiliation	Platform/language
Akuanduba-UDESC	Universidade Federal de Santa Catarina	JaCaMo
Dumping to Gather	Technical University of Berlin	ROS Hybrid Behaviour Planner
Jason-DTU	Technical University of Denmark	Jason + CArtAgO
SMART_JaCaMo	Pontifícia Universidade Católica do Rio Grande do Sul, University of Liverpool, Universidade Federal de Santa Catarina	JaCaMo
TUBDAI	Technical University of Berlin	ROS Hybrid Behaviour Planner

The results of this year's Contest are listed in Table 3. The team *SMART_JaCaMo* achieved the highest score with 33 points, closely followed by *TUBDAI* with 27 points. Due to an unclarity regarding the Contest rules, the steering committee decided to not award a first place this time, so both teams were placed second. *Jason-DTU* made a close third place with 21 points, followed by *Dumping to Gather* with 9 points. Unfortunately, *Akuanduba-UDESC* encountered severe problems during the contest and was not able to win against their opponents.

---

[8] Coincidentally, all games were played in the biggest cities of the contestants' home countries.

Table 3. Results.

Place	Team	Points	Simulations won
2	*SMART_JaCaMo*	33	11
2	*TUBDAI*	27	9
3	*Jason-DTU*	21	7
4	*Dumping to Gather*	9	3
5	*Akuanduba-UDESC*	0	–

3.3   The Teams and Their Agents

In this section, we will take a look at each individual team, what kind of frameworks and techniques they used and how much effort they invested.

SMART_JaCaMo: The biggest team in the Contest, *SMART_JaCaMo* [22], consists of 8 persons: Tabajara Krausburg, Débora C. Engelmann, Vitor Peres, Giovani P. Farias, Juliana Damasio and Rafael H. Bordini from Pontifícia Universidade Católica do Rio Grande do Sul, Rafael C. Cardoso from University of Liverpool and Jomi F. Hübner from Universidade Federal de Santa Catarina. The Brazilian team invested approximately 120 h combined for programming and all other tasks, building on their contest entry from 2017 - they competed for the third time in the Contest. The team's agents were implemented in JaCaMo [11], a framework that combines Jason [12] for agent programming, CArtAgO [23] for programming environment artifacts (e.g. for coordination) and Moise [18] to add an organisational layer to the MAS.

The team doubled their previous code base to ca. 6100 lines, half of which makes up the agent program(s). The other half falls upon configuration files and plain Java code.

The team started development for this year's Contest in April 2018. Decomposing jobs and allocating the tasks is solved with the *Contract Net Protocol*. Coordination is achieved via Moise schemes. Interestingly, agents synchronise with the server through a personal artefact, that filters percepts for the agent and is responsible for holding the agent's planned actions and relaying them to the server.

TUBDAI: The *TUBDAI* team [16] consists of only 2 people: Christopher-Eyk Hrabia and Michael Ettlinger from Technische Universität Berlin, Germany. Approximately 600 h were spent to create the around 7000 lines big agent program using the *ROS Hybrid Behaviour Planner*, a planning and decision making component for the *Robot Operating System* (ROS), developed at the DAI-Labor of TU Berlin.

TUBDAI started work in May of 2018. The *Contract Net Protocol* is again used for coordination. The agent's main strategy is to only let drones build wells in locations that cannot be reached by other roles. The other teams expected this relatively simple strategy not to be used for various reasons and thus mostly did not have any countermeasures prepared in advance, which contributed to its success.

Jason-DTU: The *Jason-DTU* team [24] from Technical University of Denmark started quite late: they only had 3 weeks until the Contest. The 5 members of *Jason-DTU* are Jørgen Villadsen, Mads Okholm Bjørn, Andreas Halkjær From, Thomas Søren Henney and John Bruntse Larsen. Their final agent program comprises around 6200 lines of code, some of it being recycled from their previous participation. As *SMART_JaCaMo*, the team also programmed their agents using the *Jason* platform. Interestingly their agent code only makes up roughly a tenth of the complete program (compared to about 50% for *SMART_JaCaMo*).

The *Jason-DTU* strategy begins by dividing the agents into 4 mostly fixed groups for resource acquisition, well dismantling, map exploration and item assembling. Completing enough jobs makes some agent switch to well building, while discovering opponent wells makes dismantling agents stop exploring and follow their original purpose. Having found a resource node for each resource type makes map exploring agents take other tasks instead and resource gatherers stop switch to dismantling wells once their main storage unit is almost full.

Dumping to Gather: The *Dumping to Gather* team [17], also from TU Berlin, used the *ROS Hybrid Behaviour Planner* as well. The team consists of 3 people: Christopher Eyk-Hrabia, Marc Schmidt and Marie Weintraud and originates from a course given at TU Berlin. As most others, the team started work in April. About 340 h were spent creating the 8600 lines strong agent program.

For each job in the simulation, one agent is appointed coordinator and (once again) uses the *Contract Net Protocol* to distribute the tasks resulting from the job. Drones are used for exploring the map. Auctions are also ignored by this team and jobs are just completed as they come, without analysing if one job might be better than another.

Akuanduba-UDESC: The second Brazilian team, *Akuanduba-UDESC* [15], consists of 5 people: Guilherme Rafael Deschamps, Tiago Funk, Vilson Junior, Giovanni Jakubiak de Albuquerque and Tiago Luiz Schmitz, all of them from Universidade Federal de Santa Catarina. As the *SMART_JaCaMo* team, they used the *JaCaMo* platform to create an agent program comprising about 4000 lines, 3000 thereof making up the Jason agent code. The team invested roughly 500 h for the Contest, of which 300 were used for programming. Making use of special *JaCaMo* features, the agents were distributed among 3 different machines.

The *Akuanduba-UDESC* agents use a *CArtAgO* artefact for task delegation. Drones are used to explore the map. Items are gathered and assembled proactively and jobs completed if enough items of the required types are available. Only trucks are used for gathering base items.

The teams' comparison is again summarised in Table 4.

Table 4. Team comparison.

	SMART_JaCaMo	TUBDAI	Jason-DTU	Dumping to Gather	Akuanduba
Team size	8	2	5	3	5
Platform	JaCaMo	RHBP	Jason + CArtAgO	RHBP	JaCaMo
Started	April	May	September	April	April
Time spent	120 h	600 h	(3 weeks)	340 h	500 h
Codebase	3100 Jason + 1200 config + 1700 Java	7000	650 Jason + 5650 Java	8600	3000 Jason + 1000 Java

Well Building. The agents of *SMART_JaCaMo* build wells at the beginning of the simulation and when they have completed a job or destroyed an opponent's well. Wells are built at the map's borders and if no agent is in that area or no agent is currently unoccupied, it might happen that wells are not built even though the team would be able to. The *TUBDAI* agents always build wells using their drones in places that other roles cannot reach. As drones are rather slow at building, the team sometimes earns money faster than it can use it for building wells. *Jason-DTU* let only their trucks build wells, as *SMART_JaCaMo* also at the map's boundaries. As they designated specific agents for well building, when they encountered a bug (which they did), no other agent could take over the responsibility and the agents had to be restarted to be able to build wells again. The agents of *Dumping to Gather*, in contrast to the other teams, prioritise completing jobs over building wells, so that currency accumulates until there are agents not occupied by any job. Looking at any simulation, we see that these agents build their wells in straight lines along the map's boundaries. *Akuanduba-UDESC* only plans to build two wells and invests the currency in upgrades instead.

Problems. *SMART_JaCaMo* claims, their agents had problems with the amount of information on the third and largest map, which they solved with more rigorous filtering. *TUBDAI* says, one of their advantages was their surprising strategy and if it would have been anticipated more, they would have been less successful. According to *Jason-DTU*, their agents were efficiently collecting items, but their static group structure could do with improvements. Also, their agents did get stuck more or less often, generating useless or empty chains of actions. As mentioned above, this was particularly impactful when it affected the designated well building agent. The *Dumping to Gather* team encountered a problem in simulations where relatively many wells could be built as they did not anticipate such configurations. Thus, their agents could have built even more wells in certain simulations. Also, the potential locations for the wells were chosen without regard for the distance to any agent of the team. The main problem for *Akuanduba-UDESC* was their well building strategy. Additionally, their agents were best only on a certain type of map.

Most of the teams say that implementing the job completion capabilities took the most development time.

Unleveraged Potential. The *SMART_JaCaMo* team did not implement bidding for auctions, which could have opened the door for even more lucrative jobs. Also, their agents only ever used one single storage facility per simulation, which could be optimised to adapt to specific situations.

The *TUBDAI* team would like to focus less on job completion, which is understandable, given that their drone agents often cannot build as fast as the other agents completed jobs. Instead, *TUBDAI* would need to improve their well defense capabilities, which they mostly did not need this time.

As mentioned above, *Jason-DTU* would need to fix some bugs first and make their agent grouping more dynamic. They would also like to improve their well placement strategy and build far away from opponent agents and prioritise locations where wells have not been discovered before.

Akuanduba-UDESC would improve their well building strategy first and foremost. Then, optimising their agent's recharge strategy so it works better on bigger maps would be next.

3.4 Errors and Stability

For each action there is an associated set of potential errors that may occur and are reported back to the agent. The failure counts over all simulations are given in Table 5.

For example, the error code `failed_wrong_facility` occurs when an agent tries to use a facility-bound action without being at one of those facilities. Only *Akuanduba-UDESC* and *Jason-DTU* encountered this error and only very few times. All in all, we see that *Akuanduba-UDESC* faced the most errors, followed by *Jason-DTU*. For *Akuanduba-UDESC*, about half of the errors were `failed_no_route`, indicating a general planning problem. For most of the teams, a lot of these errors were also accumulated in the simulation against *TUBDAI*, were their wells were not reachable by most agents. About a fourth of the errors for *Jason-DTU* were also `failed_no_route`. Half of their errors were just `failed`, which occurs when the `recharge` action fails (by design) in about 70% of cases. This indicates less of a technical problem than the decision to try the `recharge` action very often. Another frequent error for *Jason-DTU* was `failed_counterpart`, which can be the result of `give`/`receive` actions and `assist_assemble`, if the interaction with the other agent somehow failed (e.g. because the other agent is not there yet). *Jason-DTU* was the only team to see `failed_unknown_job` (12 times), which is returned if an agent tries to deliver to or bid on a job that does not exist.

Table 5. Reasons for failed actions

Reason	Akuanduba-UDESC	Dumping to Gather	Jason-DTU	TUBDAI	SMART_JaCaMo
failed_wrong_facility	24	–	39	–	–
failed_unknown_job	–	–	12	–	–
failed_job_status	425	37	164	26	–
failed_no_route	70073	30928	23598	2136	151
failed_capacity	18524	152	2833	2	–
failed_resources	2123	–	2	145	628
failed_tools	14677	16049	7693	4411	164
useless	–	182	29	55	–
failed_location	690	7658	1333	833	1093
successful_partial	4353	3512	2616	1963	2238
failed_counterpart	4742	10558	18206	7861	362
failed	4195	19909	56711	18838	27009
failed_item_amount	29164	6071	3118	1776	55
Total	148990	95056	116354	38046	31700

Dumping to Gather encountered `failed_no_route` most often, as well, followed by `failed`. It was also the only team to never get the `failed_resources` result, which only occurs if an agent attempts to build a well without having the necessary funds.

TUBDAI and *SMART_JaCaMo* had comparably few `failed_no_route` results, probably due to *TUBDAI* being responsible for the other teams getting the error and *SMART_JaCaMo* being able to cope with that. *SMART_JaCaMo* was the only team to never get the `failed_capacity` result, which occurs when items are to be transferred between agents or an agent and a storage and the target does not have enough free space. *TUBDAI* also only got this error 2 times, which is negligible, indicating very accurate resource management for both teams.

`failed_item_amount` and `failed_tools` mainly happen when not enough items or not all roles required for the assembling process are present. *SMART_JaCaMo* saw these errors way less than the other teams, pointing to very good coordination among the team's agents.

4   Interesting Simulation

In this section, we will take a closer look at one of the simulations and analyse the agents' behaviour from a bird's-eye view.

4.1 *Jason-DTU* vs. *SMART_JaCaMo* Simulation 2 of 3

Jason-DTU won against *SMART_JaCaMo* one out of 3 simulations[9]. This was the only matchup that did not end with one team winning all 3 simulations, so we would like to get an idea of why *Jason-DTU* was able to win one of the simulations. Charts for massium (the reward obtained from completing jobs) and accumulated score are given in Figs. 2 and 3 respectively.

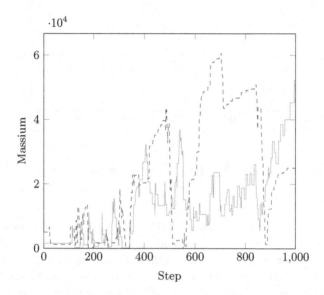

Fig. 2. *Jason-DTU* (red) vs. *SMART_JaCaMo* (blue/dashed) sim 2 - massium (Color figure online)

From the score chart, we see that *Jason-DTU* is clearly behind *SMART_JaCaMo* for a long time. Only in step 800, *Jason-DTU* pushes ahead and *SMART_JaCaMo* cannot keep up for the rest of the simulation. While *SMART_JaCaMo* starts out with much better growth, the curve flattens out, whereas the curve of *Jason-DTU* starts out rather flat and begins to grow faster around step 500. Looking at total massium earned, *Jason-DTU* lies far ahead of its opponent with 322000 compared to only 188000. Thus, *Jason-DTU* could build far more wells in this simulation. Though, *SMART_JaCaMo* was the team that had the most massium shortly after step 600 and almost spent it completely around step 800. Comparing the characteristics, we also see that *SMART_JaCaMo* seems to have phases where massium is spent, while the curve of *Jason-DTU* is wildly oscillating, meaning that massium is spent almost as soon as it is earned. Back to step 600, the score of *SMART_JaCaMo* is already

---

[9] The replay can be viewed at https://multiagentcontest.org/2018/replays/?2018-09-24-14-05-06-Contest-2018-2of3.

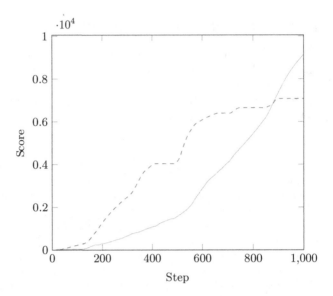

Fig. 3. *Jason-DTU* (red) vs. *SMART_JaCaMo* (blue/dashed) sim 2 - score (Color figure online)

6000 while *Jason-DTU* is still below 3000. While *SMART_JaCaMo* is earning 7 points per step, *Jason-DTU* is already at 18 though. In step 660, after having discovered the spot where *SMART_JaCaMo* built a number of wells, *Jason-DTU* manages to completely dismantle all of its opponent's wells. *SMART_JaCaMo* then spends a share of its fortune on building wells in the exact same location, while *Jason-DTU* still has wells at various locations at the map's border. Around step 850, *SMART_JaCaMo* has selected a new spot to build wells and goes up to 8 score points per step, while not bothering *Jason-DTU* much, who got to 22 score points per step in the meantime. The new spot does not last long as *Jason-DTU* almost immediately begins to dismantle the wells. This may go unnoticed (or ignored) by *SMART_JaCaMo* - the agents build even more wells in the location that is currently being attacked by *Jason-DTU*, who is sending more and more agents to dismantle until no well is left standing. Meanwhile, *SMART_JaCaMo* is mostly ignoring the wells of their opponent. Having dismantled one of these, a large group of agents passes by another two *Jason-DTU* wells without reacting to them. Now, *Jason-DTU* has surpassed *SMART_JaCaMo*, who is again at 0 points per step and makes no further attempt at building wells for the remainder of the simulation.

5 Conclusion and Outlook

We have once again seen an exciting Contest. Unfortunately, we only had 5 participating teams, one of which was struggling to play and even connected passive agents later, only to progress the simulations faster. Nonetheless, we have seen a mix of advantageous strategies and good multi-agent system engineering. For the first time in years, we had only agent-based approaches competing, 2 using *RHBP* and 3 using *Jason* plus add-ons (*CArtAgO* and/or *Moise*).

5.1 Suggestions by the Teams

We also asked the teams for feedback regarding the scenario and the Contest in general. They proposed, for example, to improve the qualification phase and put more (scenario-specific) requirements on the teams besides just sending actions in time, which, admittedly, is easy to achieve without even having a real agent team ready.

Scenario-wise, more *interaction* among the agent teams is desired. We already tried to go in this direction with the well-building aspect this year and continue on this road. Also, there is a request for more *decentralisation*. We see a need here as well, though it is very difficult to design a scenario that rewards a decentralised way of thinking - unless we restrict the amount of information that agents can share, which would also mean we would have to make sure that agents can only communicate through our infrastructure.

Generally, the teams wish for a scenario that represents "modern" challenges, while they would also like a scenario with less need for scenario-specific optimisation (i.e. the acquisition and assembling of items in the current scenario).

Another proposal is to provide the same conditions for all participants in terms of hardware and/or connection speed. Again, this would make organising the Contest a lot harder (at least in the beginning), though we are on the lookout for possible technical solutions (virtual machines, container platforms, etc.).

5.2 Contest Rules

To establish more clear-cut rules, we asked whether the teams think it should be allowed to make changes to an agent team during the contest. This is of course controversial, as a team that plays later has the chance to make changes to react on observed opponent behaviour, which a team that plays first does not have. Opinions here are unfortunately not aligned at all. Some teams think, all changes should be allowed, while others suggest the agents should be submitted before the contest, so that no changes are possible at all. Of course, this is also disadvantageous for the Contest as a whole, as it creates a lot of work for the organisers and might lead to simulations, where an unforeseen bug occurs in one of the agent teams (for example a simple typo), and leads to at least one less interesting simulation. Somewhat more balanced opinions suggest to allow only bugfix changes and either let each team's conscience decide what makes a bugfix and what does not, or let each change get approved first, e.g. by the organizers.

5.3 Plans for the Future

As usual, we plan to use a completely new scenario next time, after having established and scaled up this one two times already. While the current scenario was quite complex and interesting to solve, it was lacking a certain visibility. Looking at a simulation, the bigger picture remains mostly hidden. Only the money/score numbers give some kind of indication. The new well facilities were a first step in this direction, providing some more easily measurable features. On the other hand, the complexity of the scenario required a lot of work upfront, before the participants could see any results. We would like our next scenario to allow for simple solutions that can play it, while leaving a lot of room for advanced solutions to get even better results. The third feature, one we want to bring back again, is interaction among the teams. While in the first two iterations interaction was possible but not promoted, we already saw a little more interaction this time with teams struggling to defend their wells against their opponents. Judging from the questionnaires, the participants would still like to see more direct interaction, e.g. like in the earlier *Mars scenario*, where some agents could effectively disable agents from the opposing team.

Acknowledgement. We would like to thank Alfred Hofmann from Springer for his continuous support for more than 10 years now, and for endowing the price of 500 Euros in Springer books.

References

1. Ahlbrecht, T., et al.: Multi-agent programming contest 2013: the teams and the design of their systems. In: Cossentino, M., El Fallah Seghrouchni, A., Winikoff, M. (eds.) EMAS 2013. LNCS (LNAI), vol. 8245, pp. 366–390. Springer, Heidelberg (2013). https://doi.org/10.1007/978-3-642-45343-4_22
2. Ahlbrecht, T., Dix, J., Fiekas, N.: Multi-agent programming contest 2016. IJAOSE **6**(1), 58–85 (2018)
3. Ahlbrecht, T., Dix, J., Fiekas, N.: Multi-agent programming contest 2017. Ann. Math. Artif. Intell. **84**(1–2), 1–16 (2018)
4. Ahlbrecht, T., Dix, J., Köster, M., Schlesinger, F.: Multi-agent programming contest 2013. In: Cossentino, M., El Fallah Seghrouchni, A., Winikoff, M. (eds.) EMAS 2013. LNCS (LNAI), vol. 8245, pp. 292–318. Springer, Heidelberg (2013). https://doi.org/10.1007/978-3-642-45343-4_16
5. Ahlbrecht, T., Dix, J., Schlesinger, F.: From testing agent systems to a scalable simulation platform. In: Eiter, T., Strass, H., Truszczyński, M., Woltran, S. (eds.) Advances in Knowledge Representation, Logic Programming, and Abstract Argumentation. LNCS (LNAI), vol. 9060, pp. 47–62. Springer, Cham (2015). https://doi.org/10.1007/978-3-319-14726-0_4
6. Behrens, T., Dastani, M., Dix, J., Hübner, J., Köster, M., Novák, P., Schlesinger, F.: The multi-agent programming contest. AI Mag. **33**(4), 111–113 (2012)
7. Behrens, T., Dastani, M., Dix, J., Köster, M., Novák, P.: The multi-agent programming contest from 2005–2010: from collecting gold to herding cows. Ann. Math. Artif. Intell. **59**, 277–311 (2010)
8. Behrens, T., Dastani, M., Dix, J., Köster, M., Novák, P. (eds.): Annals of Mathematics and Artificial Intelligence, vol. 59. Springer, Netherlands (2010). Special Issue about Multi-Agent-Contest I

9. Behrens, T.M., Dastani, M., Dix, J., Novák, P.: Agent contest competition: 4th edition. In: Hindriks, K.V., Pokahr, A., Sardina, S. (eds.) ProMAS 2008. LNCS (LNAI), vol. 5442, pp. 211–222. Springer, Heidelberg (2009). https://doi.org/10.1007/978-3-642-03278-3_14

10. Behrens, T., Köster, M., Schlesinger, F., Dix, J., Hübner, J.F.: The multi-agent programming contest 2011: a résumé. In: Dennis, L., Boissier, O., Bordini, R.H. (eds.) ProMAS 2011. LNCS (LNAI), vol. 7217, pp. 155–172. Springer, Heidelberg (2012). https://doi.org/10.1007/978-3-642-31915-0_9

11. Boissier, O., Bordini, R.H., Hübner, J.F., Ricci, A., Santi, A.: Multi-agent oriented programming with JaCaMo. Sci. Comput. Program. **78**(6), 747–761 (2013)

12. Bordini, R.H., Hübner, J.F., Wooldridge, M.: Programming Multi-Agent Systems in AgentSpeak Using Jason, vol. 8. Wiley, New York (2007)

13. Dastani, M., Dix, J., Novák, P.: The second contest on multi-agent systems based on computational logic. In: Inoue, K., Satoh, K., Toni, F. (eds.) CLIMA 2006. LNCS (LNAI), vol. 4371, pp. 266–283. Springer, Heidelberg (2007). https://doi.org/10.1007/978-3-540-69619-3_15

14. Dastani, M., Dix, J., Novák, P.: Agent contest competition: 3rd edition. In: Dastani, M., El Fallah Seghrouchni, A., Ricci, A., Winikoff, M. (eds.) ProMAS 2007. LNCS (LNAI), vol. 4908, pp. 221–240. Springer, Heidelberg (2008). https://doi.org/10.1007/978-3-540-79043-3_14

15. Funk, T., Deschamps, G.R., Junior, V.D.C., de Albuquerque, G.J., Moser, P., Schmitz, T.L.: A task-oriented architecture with priority queue for BDI agents applied to the multi agent programming contest scenario. In: Ahlbrecht, T., et al. (eds.) MAPC 2018, LNAI 11957, pp. 25–40. Springer, Cham (2019)

16. Hrabia, C.-E., Ettlinger, M.F., Hessler, A.: ROS hybrid behaviour planner: behaviour hierarchies and self-organisation in the multi-agent programming contest. In: Ahlbrecht, T., et al. (eds.) MAPC 2018, LNAI 11957, pp. 120–143. Springer, Cham (2019)

17. Hrabia, C.-E., Schmidt, M., Weintraud, A.M., Hessler, A.: Distributed decision-making based on shared knowledge in the multi-agent programming contest. In: Ahlbrecht, T., et al. (eds.) MAPC 2018, LNAI 11957, pp. 101–119. Springer, Cham (2019)

18. Hübner, J.F., Sichman, J.S., Boissier, O.: $\mathcal{S}\text{-}\mathcal{M}oise^+$: a middleware for developing organised multi-agent systems. In: Boissier, O., et al. (eds.) AAMAS 2005. LNCS (LNAI), vol. 3913, pp. 64–77. Springer, Heidelberg (2006). https://doi.org/10.1007/11775331_5

19. Karakovskiy, S., Togelius, J.: The Mario AI benchmark and competitions. IEEE Trans. Comput. Intell. AI Games **4**(1), 55–67 (2012)

20. Ketter, W., Peters, M., Collins, J.: Autonomous agents in future energy markets: the 2012 power trading agent competition. In: Twenty-Seventh AAAI Conference on Artificial Intelligence (2013)

21. Köster, M., Schlesinger, F., Dix, J.: The multi-agent programming contest 2012. In: Dastani, M., Hübner, J.F., Logan, B. (eds.) ProMAS 2012. LNCS (LNAI), vol. 7837, pp. 174–195. Springer, Heidelberg (2013). https://doi.org/10.1007/978-3-642-38700-5_11

22. Krausburg, T., et al.: SMART-JaCaMo: an organisation-based team for the multi-agent programming contest. In: Ahlbrecht, T., et al. (eds.) MAPC 2018, LNAI 11957, pp. 72–100. Springer, Cham (2019)

23. Ricci, A., Piunti, M., Viroli, M., Omicini, A.: Environment programming in CArtAgO. In: El Fallah Seghrouchni, A., Dix, J., Dastani, M., Bordini, R.H. (eds.) Multi-Agent Programming, pp. 259–288. Springer, Boston (2009). https://doi.org/10.1007/978-0-387-89299-3_8
24. Villadsen, J., Bjørn, M.O., From, A.H., Henney, T.S., Larsen, J.B.: Multi-agent programming contest 2018 - the Jason-DTU team. In: Ahlbrecht, T., et al. (eds.) MAPC 2018, LNAI 11957, pp. 41–71. Springer, Cham (2019)
25. Wellman, M.P., et al.: Designing the market game for a trading agent competition. IEEE Internet Comput. **5**(2), 43–51 (2001)

The Teams

A Task-Oriented Architecture with Priority Queue for BDI Agents Applied to the Multi Agent Programming Contest Scenario

Tiago Funk[✉], Guilherme Rafael Deschamps[✉],
Vilson de Deus Corrêa Júnior[✉], Giovanni Jakubiak de Albuquerque[✉],
Paolo Moser[✉], and Tiago Luiz Schmitz[✉]

Universidade do Estado de Santa Catarina, Ibirama, Brazil
tiagoff.tf@gmail.com, guilhermerd6@hotmail.com, vilsonjrcorrea@gmail.com,
giovannijakubiak@hotmail.com, paolo.moser@udesc.br,
tiago.schmitz@udesc.br

Abstract. On 2018 we participated of a Multi-Agent Programming Contest, as *Akuanduba_UDESC* team. We matched upon Agents in the City scenario, with our agents aiming to earn money, fulfilling jobs and missions and also get points through the *wells*. To accomplish these goals we used a task-oriented architecture with a priorities queue to manage tasks, focusing on developing agents that can choose correctly which *tasks* they need to perform and change the tasks state to coordinate themselves. We did not reach a good position on the contest, mainly because of a poor strategy for the wells building, but we have saw that all those things we focused on our development returned good results (i.e. the priorities queue and the tasks manager worked successfully).

1 Introduction

The Multi-Agent Programming Contest (MAPC) [1] is a competition in which participants must identify and develop solutions for the proposed problems, showing suitable benchmarks and gathering test cases. In each round of the contest, two teams compete simultaneously with 34 agents each, divided as cars, motorcycles, drones and trucks. The teams dispute on getting points and earning money. The points acquisition occurs by the water wells, which consume money to be built by the agents, and after built generate points for each step. Each round is composed by 1000 *steps*, strategy used to systematize the progress of the simulation. To earn money the agents deliver missions and jobs, that consume basic items (that can be gathered) and assembled items (that can not be gathered). The money is utilized to upgrade the agents and the water wells building. In this paper, we will present: (i) the architecture and strategies utilized by the team *Akuanduba_UDESC* in MAPC 2018, (ii) the results of the contest (Sect. 8) and (iii) the appraisal of the team.

© Springer Nature Switzerland AG 2019
T. Ahlbrecht et al. (Eds.): MAPC 2018, LNAI 11957, pp. 25–40, 2019.
https://doi.org/10.1007/978-3-030-37959-9_2

We used a task-oriented BDI architecture (Sect. 4) on our program. Our task treating routine uses a priority queue [6]. The scheduler runs once per **step** and chooses the task with the highest priority. A task can also be set as waiting, resumed and concluded (Sect. 5). The creation of tasks is based on a process described on Sect. 6, where we explain our tasks planning. Our exceptions treatment is described in the Sect. 7. The source code for our team used in MAPC 2018 is available for download at: https://github.com/TiagoFunkUdescCeavi/ Akuanduba_MAPC_2019.

We used a task-oriented architecture because it can work on multi-agent environment, where a lot of tasks spawn all the time and the agents need to choose upon them. The main difference between *Akuanduba_UDESC* (Sect. 3) and the other teams (Sect. 2) is the priority queue.

2   Related Works

This section introduces the architectures used by some teams of the 2017 edition of MAPC. It considered the teams programming language, agents coordination and agents communication. According to Table 1 it is possible to analyze how the teams adopted centralized and/or decentralized coordination on the tasks coordination. The tasks were coordinated by teams and had the following configuration: (i) *BusyBeaver* [7] - the leader centered the tasks; (ii) *Jason-DTU* [9] - a temporary leader organized the tasks and distributed them among the agents of the groups; (iii) *lampe* [3] - the mother entity managed all the tasks and (iv) *TUBDAI* [4] - each agent was responsible by the creation of tasks. Moreover, was analyzed how they developed the communication tasks. The teams *Busy-Beaver* and *Jason-DTU* utilized the interpreter *Jason*, while *lampe* built their own infrastructure of communication infrastructure and *TUBDAI* used *ROS*.

Table 1. Architecture comparison

Team	BusyBeaver	Jason-DTU	lampe	TUBDAI
Centralized	x	x	x	x
Decentralized	-	x	-	x
Creation of tasks	Fixed Leader	Temporary Leader	Own Framework	Autonomous
Communication	Jason	Jason	Mother Ship	ROS
Language	*Python*	*Jason*	C++	*Python*

3   Akuanduba-UDESC 2018

Our team used a tasks-oriented architecture with priority queue [6] to sequence the agents actions logically. The tasks priorities are represented by numeric values, and the task with the highest value is the one with the highest priority. The Table 2 describes all the tasks with their priorities.

Table 2. Task priorities

Task	Priority	Task	Priority
recharge	10	dismantle	9.7
buildWell	9	exploration	9
mission	9	dropAll	8.9
upgradecapacity	8.5	help	8.2
craft	8	gather	8
job	5	fastgathering	4

The roles obligated the agents to fulfill one or more tasks. The artifact *CArtAgO* [8] manages the distribution of roles. The artifact is in charge to making public which role the agents assumed.

4   Infrastructure and Environment

We used a programming language called *Jason* to develop the agents. The communication with the server of the environment used *EISMassim*. The coordination between agents was made in *CArtAgO* [8]. We utilized *JADE* [2] to trade messages between agents, once they were not all running on the same machine. The agents interactions (as can be seen on the Fig. 1) was divided into agent-agent, agent-artifact and artifact-massim.

The communication artifact of the environment was the artifact *EISAccess* (Fig. 1). It provided an abstraction of game environment, allowing the agent to send actions and receive perceptions from the competition environment. In this abstraction, its observable properties are all those perceptions which the remote server sends to the agent (i.e. `jobs` state, location and *storages* state). The artifact has only one operation `action`. The operation receives the action which the agent wants to execute on environment, as a parameter.

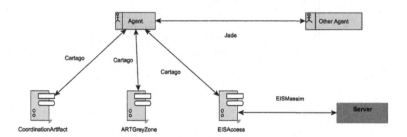

Fig. 1. Communication infrastructure

Coordination was made by `CoordinationArtifact`, that manage the agents roles. The agents manifest themselves informing the artifact their intention to assume a role. Once linked to a role the agent cannot assume any other role, and when the agent finishes its `task` it can ask for being unbinded with the paper to the artifact. An example of roles linking is to catch a specific item from a `resourceNode`. Once an item is taken on the `resourceNode`, the agent gets linked to take that item and deliver on an `storage` for all the simulation. The artifact gets in charge to manage the roles for the agents and keep the integrity, ensuring that the *tasks* will have agents enough to be fulfilled.

The `CoordinationArtifact` has observable properties. All the roles that have allocated agents are observable properties into the `CoordinationArtifact`. An observable property is only added if the agent calls on the artifact the action which makes the link between agent and `job`, and this link will be represented as an observable property on the artifact while the agent does not call the unbinding operation. Other available actions are `mission`, `gather` and `craft`, which are, respectively: (i) a special job, (ii) searching items on `resourceNodes` and (iii) items assembling using other items. Special jobs reward money like a job, otherwise it decreases the money of the team on the same value of the reward. The operations of `CoordinationArtifact` link tasks with agents and remove those links.

The linking operation works for `jobs` and `missions`. Once the agents receive the signal of new task added, they verify if themselves fulfill the requisites to complete the task and will try to compromise. The operation of the artifact will verify if the task is already being performed. If it does not, the artifact adds the task to the agent, and the agent receives a `signal` telling him to perform the task. All other agents which try to complete the same task after it is already being done will be simply ignored by the artifact (they will not receive any `signal`). On the Fig. 2 there is a sequence diagram with the steps sequence for `jobs` case.

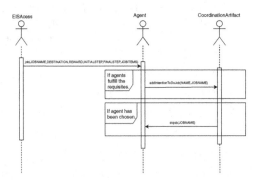

Fig. 2. Messages trading for addition of task `job`

The link-removal operation works searching for the task which the agent wants to unbind itself and once the task is found, it is removed from the list. While the link exists, there is an observable property with this information.

The gather and craft works similar, but the link is made when the simulation begin and stands until it ends, because the agent will keep performing this task (there are no gather and craft link-removal operations). The last operation of the artifact is related to tasks-linking. It removes all links that are kept when simulation ends.

The agents that assume the craft task were chosen by a mathematical model. 12 agents are responsible for the craft. The number was chosen after tests - 12 was a number of agents able to keep the storage full. The 12 agents were divided for each item that already existed, providing more agents to the items which were the most used. This quantity is computed by the formula 1, where d_i is the dependence value of the item and q_i is the quantity.

$$q_i = \left\lceil 12 \times \frac{d_i}{\sum\limits_{i \in I} d_i} \right\rceil \tag{1}$$

The most utilized items are defined by a dependence rule. We can use, as example, an item α, with its dependence represented by a numeric value consisting of how many items depend of α to be assembled. If its value is 0 $alpha$ has not dependents. Otherwise, if its value is 1, there is one item which depends of α to be assembled, and so on.

The last operation of the artifact was *informDronePositionAndCorners*, that tells the agents which will explore the environment for which part of map they should go to reduce the distance between all quadrants. The exploration consists of going through the map searching for the resourceNodes and *wells*. We split the map on 4 quadrants of the same size and analyzed each one by a drone agent. When all drone agents report their positions to the artifact, it solves a binary linear programming problem that minimize the total distance verified by the 4 drones, respecting 1 drone per quadrant [5]. The model of the problem is described on 2, where: "A" is the agents set; "C" is the quadrants set; "$\Delta(a,c)$" is the distance between agent "a" and quadrant "c" . The result of the equation returns a signal for the agent, telling which quadrant it should occupy.

$$Minimize \sum_{(a,c) \in (A \times C)} i_{(a,c)} \Delta(a,c)$$

$$s.t.$$

$$\sum_{(a,c) \in (A)} i_{(a,c)} = 1, c \in C$$

$$\sum_{(a,c) \in (C)} i_{(a,c)} = 1, a \in A \tag{2}$$

The *ARTGreyZone* artifact was the builder of the threshold zone. It is defined as the total area of the maps minus the area of the biggest convex polygon

(BCP) made by those installations which agents found on the beginning of the simulation. Threshold zone is used for *wells* building. This strategy was chosen to build the *wells* as far as possible of other installations, reducing the chances of any agent passing near the *well*.

ARTGreyZone managed add installation coordinates operation, that saves the latitude and longitude of the installation into a list. The artifact has also a cleaning memory operation that excludes the polygon.

The artifact has a polygon calculate action, which is described in the algorithm 1. Initially, the most extreme points between all the points informed by the agents are computed. The algorithm begins by searching for the most northerly point (the one that has the highest latitude coordinate). Once chosen, the point is excluded from the points list. The procedure is repeated for the most western, southern and eastern points. The search is focused in extreme points because: as bigger the approximation area, more points will be inside the polygon, reducing the iterations that will be necessary to relax the found solution. With the 4 most extreme points already chosen, the north-west, west-south, south-east and east-north points are linked by line segments to create the first approximation of BCP.

For each one of others p points in the list it is necessary to compare them with the central point of the polygon related to all its e edges. This comparison consists of calculating one determinant between the initial and final points of the e edge and the p point and calculating one determinant between the initial and final points of the e edge and the central point. Because the alignment calculation between point and straight line returns a value different than zero when there is not an alignment, the calculated value indicates on which side of the straight line is the point. So, if the signal of the straight line and central point determinant is different of the point and straight line determinant, it means that the points are on different sides of the straight line. When it happens, the current p point is added to the polygon. The addition works by removing the e edge and creating two new edges: one between the initial point of the e edge and the p point, and other between the final point of e edge and the central point.

For the agents messages trading, we used the framework *JADE* [2]. The message send is made by the *Jason* internal function .`send`. This function sends messages between agents, and because we used *JADE* infrastructure, the *Jason* language grants internally that the message will be sent for the right agent, even if it is on another machine.

The messages that we used were called **achieve** and **tell**. The **achieve** calls an action on the agent which received the message just like if it had received an order to execute a determined plan. The **tell** represents the addition of a belief on the receiver agent. The receiver agent decides what to do with this belief. In this our context, the agent executes a plan.

As an example of the .`send` using, we will describe how agents coordinate to build an item on the **craft** task. The a agent (Fig. 3) sends a message `help(WORKSHOP,PID)` - of type **achieve** - with WORKSHOP being the **workshop** where agents will meet to **craft** and PID is the identifier value of the help order,

Algorithm 1. Biggest convex polygon building

```
 1: function BUILDPOLYGON(listOfPoints)
 2:     {(x_n, y_n), (x_o, y_o), (x_s, y_s), (x_l, y_l)} ← searchCardinalPoints(listOfPoints)
 3:     polygon ← buildInitialPolygon({(x_n, y_n), (x_o, y_o), (x_s, y_s), (x_l, y_l)})
 4:     x_c ← (x_n + x_s)/2
 5:     y_c ← (y_o + y_l)/2
 6:     for all (x_p, y_p) ∈ (listOfPoints) − {(x_n, y_n), (x_o, y_o), (x_s, y_s), (x_l, y_l)} do
 7:         for all (x_1, y_1, x_2, y_2) ∈ polygon do
 8:             dC ← | x_c y_c 1 ; x_1 y_1 1 ; x_2 y_2 1 |
 9:             dP ← | x_p y_p 1 ; x_1 y_1 1 ; x_2 y_2 1 |
10:             dC ← dC / |dC|
11:             dP ← dP / |dP|
12:             if dP ≠ dC then
13:                 removeEdge(x_1, y_1, x_2, y_2)
14:                 addEdge(x_1, y_1, x_p, y_p)
15:                 addEdge(x_p, y_p, x_2, y_2)
16:             end if
17:         end for
18:     end for
19: end function
```

Where the determinant expressions are:

$$dC \leftarrow \begin{vmatrix} x_c & y_c & 1 \\ x_1 & y_1 & 1 \\ x_2 & y_2 & 1 \end{vmatrix}$$

$$dP \leftarrow \begin{vmatrix} x_p & y_p & 1 \\ x_1 & y_1 & 1 \\ x_2 & y_2 & 1 \end{vmatrix}$$

utilized to keep integrity and avoid agents to answer wrong orders. Once `help` message get received, `b` agent will calculate the cost to perform the task and help `a` agent. This calculation is done taking on account the distance between its current position and the position of the WORKSHOP. Once the calculation gets finished, `b` sends a message `helper(PID,COST)` - of type `tell` - to `a` agent, with PID being the identifier of the task and COST the calculated cost to perform the task.

Agent `a`, after receiving `helper` messages from at least 2 agents, chooses the one who reported the lowest cost and all other agents who answered the `help` message will be disposed of the task. The chosen agent receives from agent `a` a message `confirmeHepl(WORKSHOP,WHONEED)` - of type `achieve` - with WORKSHOP being the destiny of the task and WHONEED the name of the agent who needs help. `b` agent, once receiving the message, will add a new task on its own beliefs base with the information of the task. When `a` already made its choice it automatically dispose any agent that its cost it. Disposed agents receive a message `dismissHelp` and get unbinded of this help task.

5 Tasks Manager

AKUANDUBA_UDESC architecture of the agent used a tasks manager, that determined which task would have execution time on each step. Tasks manager

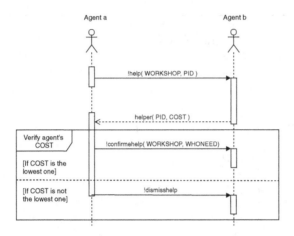

Fig. 3. Help messages

behaviour is represented in Fig. 4. Working by cycles, the process begins choosing the most priority task on that step. Once a task gets chosen, it is necessary to verify if there was tasks preemption. If a preemption occurred, the last valid state of the current task get saved to be resumed exactly where it got stopped, in the future. Saving the last valid state is named rollback. After the validation, a step of the chosen task is performed. If the step is successfully performed it gets consumed on the task. If there are no more steps to be consumed, then the task is finished.

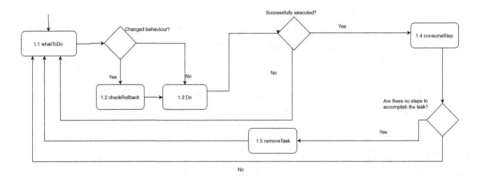

Fig. 4. Tasks manager

Tasks utilized by the tasks manager are represented as a belief `task(LABEL,PRIORITY,ACTIONS,EXECUTEDACTIONS)`, with `LABEL` being the name of the task, `PRIORITY` being the priority of the tasks (task priorities values can be seen on the Table 2), `ACTIONS` being a list containing the actions necessary to perform the task and `EXECUTEDACTIONS` being the actions that the agent have already executed. The first term of the list is the last step executed by the agent. When a new task is presented to the agent, it is added to its beliefs base. When a new task choice is made by the manager, this task can be chosen if it has the highest priority.

The lastAction(LA) is a server property that indicates which was the last action the agent tried to execute on server. The lastActionResult(LAR) indicates if the last action executed by the agent on server was successful or it failed. If failed, it indicates the type of failure. The doing(D) is a belief which indicates the name of the task which the agent compromised itself and is performing at the moment. The lastDoing(LD) is a belief developed by the agent, to know which the task was performed on the previous step. The goto is an action that can be performed by the server and it exists to allow the agent to move by the environment. When goto is executed, the agent receives a list with pairs of coordinates that represents the path that the agent needs to follow to arrive on its destiny.

The step is an observable property of the server that indicates the current step of the execution and it is updated by the server whenever a new step begins. The tasks manager plan is called by the observable property step and it is composed of 3 plans: consumeStep, whatToDo and do.

The consumeStep is the first stage of the plan, because the result of the executed action on the previous step is required. This plan consumes the executed action of the task if its execution according to the lastActionResult belief was successfully. The task belief performed on the last step gets updated, removing the first element of the ACTIONS list and adding it to the first position of EXECUTEDACTIONS list. If this action result returns failure, the agent needs to try again on future.

The second stage of the tasks manager plan is whatToDo, which verifies if there is anything to the agent perform. If there are *tasks*, the one with the highest priority gets chosen, inserting into doing belief the LABEL of the task. If the agent has not a new task to perform, it keeps idle.

When the whatToDo plan is getting finished, the plan checkRollBack is called. The checkRollBack plan verifies if there was any preemption through the doing and lastDoing beliefs. When a preemption happens, the last valid state gets restored by the rollback plan, recuperating it for the current steps sequence of the task. Saving the last state of the tasks is important to ensure that the agent will be on the right place when it is called again.

The do plan executes the next action in the ACTIONS list of the chosen task. The execution is performed sending an action to the server.

6   Tasks Planning

The list of actions needed to complete the task is settled into the task itself, when it is created. Each task that the agent can do (recharge battery, perform job, gather items in resourceNodes, etc.) has a basic actions sequence that the agent needs to perform to complete the task. In the same kind of task, the actions can change how many times it needs to be performed. Arguments of the action also can change (i.e. the `gather` task can tell the agent to collect the item 1, or the task can tell it to collect the item 3 - it depends on the argument of the action).

Using the tasks manager results in obtaining the tasks execution plan before starting its execution. To respect this characteristic, our agents build "on the fly" the plans to the tasks they want to realize.

The `gather` task consists by pick up items in the `resourceNodes` and take them to the chosen `storage`. The task can be divided into three parts: (i) go to the `resourceNode`, (ii) collect items until the charge capacity is filled and (iii) discharge the items in the central storage. To create a collect plan is necessary to tell which one is the item, where it can be found and where it needs to be left. Each item has a weight, thus it is also necessary to calculate how many elements the agent can carry. When the plan gets ready a new task is generated. Just like there is a plan to prepare the `gather` task, there is also a plan for each task (Table 2) that the agent can assume.

7   Exceptions

An exceptions control system was added to the agents to avoid them staying blocked if an action failed. The exceptions act upon situations that cannot be predicted when it will occur. All the treated errors happen when the agent tries to perform an action on the environment, but it is not a valid action or it has invalid arguments.

The first exception occurs when an agent tries to perform the `store` action and it is linked with the task download items (`dropAll`). Is needed to inform the quantity of items that the agent is carrying and wants to deliver to performs the action `store`. If this number is informed wrong, the exception `failed_item_amount` occurs. The action that is executed, to correct the agent failure, is to remove the `dropAll` task, because the agent have already fulfilled its objective.

The next exception occurs when the agent executes the action `dismantle`. If the agent tries to dismantle a well where actually there is not any well, the exception `failed_location` occurs. If this exception happened, the agent which tried the `dismantle` understands that there is not a well anymore. Predictive modeling can failure because the well can already have suffered the `dismantle` action by other agents.

The third exception may occur when an agent tries to increase its charge capacity by the action `failed_resources` while in the plan `upgradecapacity`. The `upgradecapacity` is a task which the agent performs to increase its charge capacity and costs money of the team to execute. The exception happens when the team has not enough money to pay for the upgrade. The action that corrects this error is not performing the `upgradecapacity`.

The last exception happens when the agent tries to carry more items than its charge capacity allows. The tasks planning can not predict this exception, because it can occurs when the agent carries items on its compartment and then begin trying to take others, bursting the capacity, causing the `failed_capacity`. The solution we found is the agent perform `dropAll` to empty its lading and restart charging items.

8   Results

Regarding the results of the competition, we lost the 4 matches but the technologies and techniques we used sensed a satisfactory performance. Our team acquired a lot of money by delivering `jobs`, but because as strategy error the money did not get converted to wells, finishing the matches with much money and few points. On the next paragraphs, we will make an appraisal about each relevant topic which was developed into the source code.

The agents that were designated to search for items on `resourceNodes`[1] fulfilled their task, maintaining the `storage` fully stocked during the match. During the `craft` task, which consists of items building using basic items and needs two agents in cooperation, also fulfilled their task: all items were produced and the `storage` was kept full for all the time. The `jobs` delivery were partially succeeded, because it could delivered more `jobs` during the simulation. Finally, the wells building and destruction were inefficient, with a low quantity of agents allocated to these tasks. Because of that our team got much money, but did not spend it for the wells building.

Using the tasks manager with the tasks planner was an efficient strategy to add behaviours. The code was structured in order that the main file of the agent has the manager and `imports` other files, each one treating a new behaviour. Structuring the code this way allowed us including, removing and changing agents functionalities "on the fly", creating some functionalities variations.

Table 3. Comparison between 2017 edition participant teams architectures and ours.

Team	BusyBeaver	Jason-DTU	Lampe	TUBDAI	Akuanduba UDESC
Centralized	x	x	x	x	X
Decentralized	-	x	-	x	X
Creation of tasks	Fixed Leader	Temporary Leader	Mother Ship	Autonomous	Autonomous respecting the roles
Communication	Jason	Jason	Mother Ship	ROS	JADE
priority queue	-	X	-	-	X
Predictive Modeling	-	-	X	-	X
Tasks Manager	-	-	X	-	X
Language	Python	Jason	C++	Python	Jason

---

[1] These items comprise the logistics chain base.

The use of a distributed system on three machines did not presented any disadvantages, from a technical point of view. However we had problems with the server communication because of network instability and the agents did not get to return to the match successfully.

On the Table 3 there is a comparison between some teams that enjoyed the competition in the previous year and the *Akuanduba_UDESC* team. We utilized a centralized tasks coordination and a priority queue just like the *Jason-DTU* team. We also used tasks planning and tasks manager like the *lampe* team.

A   Team Overview: Short Answers

A.1   Participants and Their Background

What was your motivation to participate in the contest?
Our professor Schmitz had already joined MAPC before and he wished to introduce the contest into our university. He chosen some students to participate with him allowing us to have a different programming experience.

What is the history of your group? (course project, thesis, ...)
Our group is composed by members of a researching project coordinated by professor Schmitz. Until 2017, the project focused on how to use multi-agent systems to coordinate autonomous aerial vehicles to analyse the Auto Vale do Itajaí hydrography. Starting in 2018, we began focusing to MAPC contest and studying the multi-agent language Jason and the framework *JaCaMo*.

What is your field of research? Which work therein is related?
The professor Schmitz has masters and doctorate in multi-agents area and the students began studying multi-agents in early 2018.

A.2   Development

How much time did you invest in the contest for programming vs. other tasks (for example organization)?
We utilized approximately 300 h for the programming, and near by 200 h focusing on other tasks.

creating vs. optimizing your agents?
We spent approximately 150 h for the agents creation. The optimizing task demanded more work, requiring approximately 350 h.

How many lines of code did you produce for your final agent team?
3093 lines on Jason
1062 lines on Java

How many people were involved and to which degree?
4 undergraduate students and 1 doctor.

When did you start working on your agents?
April, 2018.

A.3   System Details

How do your agents work together? (coordination, information sharing, ...)

Our agents were developed on Jason language and *JaCaMo* framework. The agents communicate themselves and coordinate through messages trading, sending help requests to fulfill tasks. Regarding the agents tasks attribution we utilized a *CArtAgO* artifact to perform a centralized distribution.

What are critical components of your team?

All the agents have a tasks manager, which maintains the integrity of the tasks the agents need to perform.

Can your agents change their behavior during runtime? If so, what triggers the changes?

After started, there is not any change on agents behaviour.

Did you have to make changes to the team (e.g. fix critical bugs) during the contest?

No, we did not made any change.

How do you organize your agents? Do you use e.g. hierarchies? Is your organization implicit or explicit?

We made a separation by roles. A drone agent, for example, accomplish a specific kind of task. There are also some agents who have special `jobs`, like performing a calculation or deciding who will fulfill a task.

Is most of your agents' behavior emergent on an individual or team level?

The recharge behavior of the agents is on an individual level, because it ignores every call while it is going to recharge. All other tasks were planned on team level.

If your agents perform some planning, how many steps do they plan ahead?

Once the agent receives a task it plans through a steps list how the task will be accomplished. The quantity of steps they plan ahead depends of each task. For the agents who have more than one task, each task has its own priority. So, the agent is only reactive by choosing which task it will perform, selecting the one with the highest priority.

If you have a perceive-think-act cycle, how is it synchronized with the server?

The artifact *EISAccess* receives information of the server. Whenever the agent realizes change in the `step` observable property, the thinking cycle gets triggered.

How did you go about debugging your system?

We used console messages.

Which operating system did you use, and is your team portable to other operating systems?

We used Windows. Since *JaCaMo* framework is made upon Java, the system is portable to other operating systems without changes.

What hardware did you use to run your agent team? (RAM, CPU, disk space, multiple computers, any other notable requirements)

We used three computers, each one with 16 GB RAM, and processor Intel Core i7-4770 CPU @ 3.40 GHz 3.40 GHz. Each computer was running a part of the agents, and only one was running the *CArtAgO* environment.

A.4   Scenario and Strategy

What is the main strategy of your agent team?
At the beginning, drone agents scan the map to find out the positions of all the installations (that still can not be seen in map). Meanwhile, other agents begin searching for basic items (items which do not need to be crafted). When items quantity is high enough, the agents begin the composed items crafting (items that can not be gathered in `resourceNodes`). The agents are responsible by the `jobs`. Once they realize that all the required items for one job are available on the central storage an agent complete this job. About the wells: an agent was in charge of searching for and destroying enemy wells, while two agents was building new wells.

How do your agents decide which `jobs` to complete?
Once the agents receive a job, they verify to find out if all the items required by the job are available on the central storage. If so, the job is performed, otherwise it is ignored by the agents.

Do you have different strategies for the different roles?
Yes, the drones are responsible to initially make a map sweep. A part of the trucks has obligations with the basic items, and a motorcycle has aim to destroy wells. The remaining agents divide themselves into items builders, builder helpers and job delieverers.

Do your agents form ad-hoc teams to complete a task?
We separated our agents by agent types performing determined tasks. For example, drones (and only drones) wwew performing the map sweep, trucks (and only trucks) were collecting basic items.

How do your agents decide when and where to build wells?
We catched all the points containing installations and the most distant points of the center were used to create the biggest convex polygon. From them we calculated the threshold zone, composed by the map totality less the region of the biggest convex polygon. We used This area to build two wells.

If your agents accumulated a lot of currency, why did they not spend it immediately?
Because our strategy was composed by building only two wells so the most part of the money was spent only on upgrades.

A.5   And the Moral of it is ...

What did you learn from participating in the contest?
We learnt the framework *JaCaMo*, the multi-agents oriented paradigm and mainly analyse and develop a multi-agents system with a strong coordination between agents.

What are the strong and weak points of your team?

Our agents were efficient producing items and delivering jobs, but we failed on creating wells task. The strong points of our team were that we had an efficient allocation of tasks to the members of the team. The weak points was that we had minimal knowledge on the utilized language and about the operation of the contest. Communication among the failed sometimes. We also experienced resistance and troubles by using the Version Control System (VCS).

How viable were your chosen programming language, methodology, tools, and algorithms?

The *JaCaMo* framework was chosen exactly because it embraces the development of multi-agents systems. Using the *ojalgo* library helped us on the optimization tasks. The set of utilized features (*JaCaMo*, *ojalgo*, *Eclipse*) was suitable for the system development.

Did you encounter new problems during the contest?

Yes, our agents were optimized for a specific map and failed for others utilized on the contest. We had also troubles with network instability.

Did playing against other agent teams bring about new insights on your own agents?

Yes, we noticed our bad exploitation of money for producing wells.

What would you improve if you wanted to participate in the same contest a week from now (or next year)?

We would add into our strategy the creation of more wells and optimize our agents battery recharge algorithm for the biggest maps.

Which aspect of your team cost you the most time?

Developing the tasks manager. Once it was concluded all the others tasks had a similar time spent (among them).

Why did your team perform as it did? Why did the other teams perform better/worse than you did?

Our wells build strategy failed and the other teams reached a better position than ours because they had a more consistent strategy. On the other hand, our strategy was focused on obtaining a lot of items and money. On this point we had an efficient performance.

A.6   The Future of the MAPC

What can be improved regarding the contest for next year?

Optimize the map interface to turn easier viewing the data of each element. For example, the implementation of a field where one may type the name of an agent and automatically selected it.

What kind of scenario would you like to play next? What kind of features should the new scenario have?

We have no idea.

Should the teams be allowed to make changes to their agents during the contest (even based on opponent agent behavior observed in earlier matches)? If yes, should only some changes be legal and

which ones (e.g. bugfixes), and how to decide a change's classification? If no, should we ensure that no changes are made and how?
We are not in favor of changing the agents after the contest beginning, including bugs.

Do you have ideas to reduce the impact of unforeseen strategies (e.g., playing a second leg after some time)?
If an unforeseen strategy causes a loss in the match, then the responsible team loses the match.

References

1. Ahlbrecht, T., Dix, J., Fiekas, N.: Multi-agent programming contest 2017. Ann. Math. Artif. Intell. **84**(1), 1–16 (2018)
2. Bellifemine, F.L., Caire, G., Greenwood, D.: Developing Multi-agent Systems with JADE, vol. 7. Wiley, Hoboken (2007)
3. Czerner, P., Pieper, J.: Multi-agent programming contest 2017: lampe team description. Ann. Math. Artif. Intell. **84**(1–2), 95–115 (2018)
4. Hrabia, C.E., Lehmann, P.M., Battjbuer, N., Hessler, A., Albayrak, S.: Applying robotic frameworks in a simulated multi-agent contest. Ann. Math. Artif. Intell. **84**, 117–138 (2018)
5. Longaray, A.A., Beuren, I.M.: Cálculo de minimização dos custos de produção por meio da programação linear (2001)
6. de Oliveira, R.S.: Escalonamento de tarefas imprecisas em ambiente distribuído (1997)
7. Pieper, J.: Multi-agent programming contest 2017: busybeaver team description. Ann. Math. Artif. Intell. **84**, 17–33 (2018)
8. Ricci, A., Viroli, M., Omicini, A.: CArtAgO: a framework for prototyping artifact-based environments in MAS. In: Weyns, D., Parunak, H.V.D., Michel, F. (eds.) E4MAS 2006. LNCS (LNAI), vol. 4389, pp. 67–86. Springer, Heidelberg (2007). https://doi.org/10.1007/978-3-540-71103-2_4
9. Villadsen, J., Fleckenstein, O., Hatteland, H., Larsen, J.B.: Engineering a multi-agent system in Jason and CArtAgO. Ann. Math. Artif. Intell. **84**, 57–74 (2018)

Multi-Agent Programming Contest 2018—The Jason-DTU Team

Jørgen Villadsen[✉], Mads Okholm Bjørn, Andreas Halkjær From,
Thomas Søren Henney, and John Bruntse Larsen

Algorithms, Logic and Graphs Section,
Department of Applied Mathematics and Computer Science,
Technical University of Denmark,
Richard Petersens Plads, Building 324, 2800 Kongens Lyngby, Denmark
jovi@dtu.dk

Abstract. We provide a brief description of the Jason-DTU system, including the overall system design and the tools that we used in the Multi-Agent Programming Contest. We also provide a detailed evaluation of our system. The strengths of our system include dynamic assignment of agents to groups, enabling flexible use of agents according to the current situation. Our team performed overall very well and we won some matches by either a fairly big margin or closely.

1 Introduction

In the present paper we provide a brief description of the Jason-DTU system that we used in the Multi-Agent Programming Contest (MAPC).

For MAPC 2017 we developed our multi-agent system using two frameworks, namely Jason [1], a Java-based interpreter for an extended version of AgentSpeak; and CArtAgO [2], a common artifact infrastructure for agents open environments, cf. [9]:

- Jason implements the operational semantics of AgentSpeak, and provides a platform for the development of multi-agent systems, including several customizable features. The extended version of AgentSpeak is a logic based agent-oriented programming language with Prolog-like syntax, allowing for succinct agent logic.
- CArtAgO is a general purpose framework/infrastructure that facilitates the programming of virtual environments for multi-agent systems. The framework is based on the Agents & Artifacts meta-model, introducing high-level metaphors taken from human cooperative working environments such as *agents*, *artifacts* and *workspaces*. Artifacts are resources and tools, which can be dynamically constructed, used and manipulated by agents to realize their individual or collective goals.

T. Ahlbrecht et al. (Eds.): MAPC 2018, LNAI 11957, pp. 41–71, 2019.
https://doi.org/10.1007/978-3-030-37959-9_3

For MAPC 2018 we again developed our multi-agent system using the Jason and CArtAgO frameworks. In particular CArtAgO provided an implementation of the contract net protocol that we could use to assign missions to agents. We employ an item reservation system so that agents can reserve items before they retrieve them. We also employ dynamic groups with designated responsibilities, which allow agents to coordinate in a flexible manner suitable to the situation at hand. Our team proved to be reliable, scoring well in most matches and winning some matches by either a fairly big margin or closely. In addition we identify key weaknesses in our system that we discovered during the contest, where we ended at an overall third place.

The name of our team is Jason-DTU. We participated in the contest in 2009 and 2010 as the Jason-DTU team [3,4], in 2011 and 2012 as the Python-DTU team [5,6], in 2013 and 2014 as the GOAL-DTU team [7], in 2015/2016 as the Python-DTU team [8] and in 2017 as the Jason-DTU team [9].

The members of the team are as follows:

- Jørgen Villadsen, PhD
- Mads Okholm Bjørn, MSc student
- Andreas Halkjær From, MSc student
- Thomas Søren Henney, MSc student
- John Bruntse Larsen, PhD student

We are affiliated with DTU Compute (short for Department of Applied Mathematics and Computer Science, Technical University of Denmark (DTU) and located in the greater Copenhagen area).

The main contact is associate professor Jørgen Villadsen, DTU Compute (email: jovi@dtu.dk). We invested approximately 300 man hours until the tournament started. Further details about the previous DTU teams are available here:

https://people.compute.dtu.dk/jovi/MAS/

2   System Analysis and Design

The main strategy of the team is as follows. At the beginning of each round we locate the storage and workshop facilities that are closest to each other. These are then used for the rest of the match as the *designated* storage facility and workshop.

Groups. We partition the agents into specific groups. Some of these groups are fixed for the duration of the match, and some are adjusted dynamically based on the current situation. There are six different groups:

Scouts. Initially responsible for discovering the locations of resource nodes. Most scouts are then moved into other groups except a single drone, which is used to hopefully locate enemy wells. This group initially consists of all drones and four motorcycles.

Deliverers. Their only responsibility is to deliver jobs. This group initially consists of two motorcycles, two cars, and one truck. Three drones are added after scouting ends.

Builders. Responsible for building wells. This group is managed dynamically so that more agents are added to it when enough massium has been acquired to build the desired well type. Agents are then removed from it and put back in their original group after the well is constructed.

Destroyers. These agents, initially three trucks, are responsible for discovering and destroying enemy wells. Destroyers may be turned into builders.

Gatherers. These agents gather the resource that is currently most in demand and store it in the storage facility for use by other agents. Gatherers may be turned into builders. This group initially consists of every agent not allocated to the other groups. If at some point we have enough items for the rest of the match, gatherers will be turned into destroyers.

Assemblers. There are two types of assemblers: Primary assemblers and assistants. The primary assemblers consist of three trucks. These trucks take resources from the storage facility and carry them to the workshop where the assistants are waiting. There are always three assistants; one of each other role. The primary assembler then uses the items it is carrying to assemble compound items and the assistants assist it in doing so. This way, all the required roles are always present for assembly (as *all* roles are always present).

Scouting. When the match begins, the primary assemblers move to the storage facility to wait for resources and the assistants move to the workshop. The scouts, in fact all agents, share a view of what parts of the map have been explored. Scouts keep moving to the nearest unexplored part of the city until one of each type of resource node has been located. Three drone scouts then turn into deliverers and the other types of scouts turn into gatherers.

Assembling. When the scouting phase is complete, the agents start accumulating resources in the storage facility, and the assemblers start the assembly process. The goal is to always have some of each type of item available, so that we can theoretically deliver any job. To accomplish this goal, the primary assemblers consider all assembled items that we still do not have in storage and pick one. To avoid picking the same item, assemblers share an index that is then incremented. If the required items for that item are not present in the storage and some of them require assembly, we set out to assemble these lower-tier items first instead. The number of items to assemble depends on the volume of the required items compared to the capacity of the primary assembler as well as how much we have in stock. Items are always built from immediate components as this is most likely more efficient in terms of capacity; that is, we ensure that primary assemblers always carry only direct dependencies. When primary assemblers want to assemble an item, they request this publicly. In every round, the assistant assemblers assist the first primary assembler that requests help. Because the primary assemblers also spend time driving back and forth between the storage and the workshop, this simple mechanism seems to work well in practice, and starvation is not a problem.

It is important to clarify what we mean when we say an item is present in the storage. To avoid that assemblers/deliverers steal items from each other, so that items they expected to be there have been snatched when they arrive, we employ a reservation system. When an assembler commits to assembling a number of items, it reserves the required components in the storage. Then, when other agents consider what is in storage, reserved items are subtracted from the actual stock. Because the reservations are implemented as a counter for each type of item, agents "unreserve" the items again when they retrieve them.

This reservation system has the added benefit of making gatherers more efficient: When choosing which resource to gather next, they take reservations into account so that the most needed items are gathered first. They then pick the nearest known resource node to gather from and gather until capacity before delivering at the storage.

Delivery. When a job comes in, we check the storage to see if the required items are all present. If they are not, the job is ignored. If they are, the items are reserved and available deliverers bid internally on how much of the job they can deliver and how fast. Being able to deliver all of the job is prioritized over doing it quickly, but speed is used to break ties. The winning agents then commit to picking up the items at the storage and delivering them to the required facility. When done, they return to the facility and re-deposit any undelivered items in case the delivery was unsuccessful.

Well Building. We now turn to the behaviour of the well builders. The desired type of well is calculated based on what we can afford and the integrity and efficiency of the available types. Then when we have enough massium to build a well, we look through all gatherers and destroyers that are trucks and not currently in the process of building a well and see which one is closest to the map periphery. This agent becomes a well builder which means that it will plot a route to the nearest point on the periphery, fully build a well there, and return to its current task. We use trucks to build wells because they can do it quickly. We never rebuild wells if they are being destroyed. Several drawbacks of this well strategy were discovered during the competition and will be discussed below.

Well Destruction. The well destroyers continuously explore random parts of the periphery of the map, possibly by travelling across it. When the location of an enemy well is discovered (by anyone) this is broadcast to all well destroyers who then collectively go there to destroy that well. In the event that a well has already been targeted, the destruction of the newly discovered well is delayed until the current target is gone, no matter how many destroyers are actually free or how far away the wells are. This weakness is discussed under item Sect. 3.2.

End Game. Finally we turn to what we call the end game. Once we have filled the main storage to 85% of its capacity (more on this cutoff under item Sect. 3.2), we estimate that it will contain enough resources to last the rest of the game. At this point we turn all gatherers into destroyers to be able to destroy as many enemy wells as possible as quickly as possible. The fact that destroying enemy wells earns you massium makes this even more worthwhile. The destroyers are still temporarily turned into well builders when required.

2.1   Remarks

We do not use any existing MAS methodology like Prometheus, O-MaSE, or Tropos.

Everything runs on a single machine.

We do not coordinate everything through a single agent, but some decisions are centrally coordinated. An example is what jobs to solve, which is decided by a single agent based on current stock, and then available deliverers decide among each other who should deliver which items based on an auction system. Once this is decided, the agents move completely autonomously, picking their own route, planning charging on the way etc.

Gatherers choose independently which resource to gather next, but the decision is based on centralized information of how much of each type is in stock.

Destroyers also coordinate what well to destroy next.

In general, big decisions such as job selection and major pieces of information such as current stock are centrally coordinated and shared, but each agent enacts its own role, whether gathering or building a well, without coordinating with others.

The communication and coordination strategy in the agent team is determined by the fact that information is shared by the agents running in the same Java process on different threads.

Coordination of which primary assembler to assist is thus implemented as a flag that is updated accordingly in each simulation step by the first to ask for help. This could, and maybe should, also have been done using message passing in AgentSpeak.

Decisions on who to deliver which parts of a job are implemented using the contract net protocol provided by CArtAgO. This is implemented through an artifact that accepts bids and notifies the bidders on whether they won or not.

The key agent features *autonomy*, *proactiveness* and *reactiveness* are implemented as follows:

Autonomy. Each agent runs in its own Java thread with its own AgentSpeak loop. As such, each agent has its completely own beliefs, desires and goals that it acts on. Decisions are based on these beliefs and goals which can be changed by percepts or by announcements by the other agents, but the decisions are made autonomously.

Proactiveness. Our job solving strategy is decidedly proactive: We try to build up a storage of all kinds of items such that we can solve any type of job when it arrives. On the agent level, agents will automatically incorporate charging stops into a planned route, if that route otherwise leaves them with too little charge on arrival. This (mostly) prevents the unfortunate situation of getting stuck by running out of battery. The feature is implemented in AgentSpeak as a condition on the route planning goal achievement.

Reactiveness. Agent actions may fail randomly so it is important to be able to handle that. We do this by making sure to repeat an action if the server responded with such a failure. This is also done using conditions in AgentSpeak where e.g. an action is repeated until the latest action result is the desired one.

2.2 Software Architecture

The system is implemented in Jason with CArtAgO for communication and coordination. Actions are written in Java and the agent loops are written in AgentSpeak that call the Java operations.

We developed on Linux and macOS using IntelliJ IDEA. The system was deployed on a Windows machine during the competition.

We use CArtAgO to provide common artifact infrastructure to the agents, as well as the runtime platform provided by Jason.

2.3 Main Algorithms

Since we did not get the locations of the resource nodes in the map initially, the first order of business was to locate at least one of each type of resource node. To keep track of which parts of the map we had already discovered, we split the map into a discrete grid of small squares, where each square has either been searched or not. The grid is kept up to date by marking all squares within an agents vision as searched each time we receive an update to an agents position. About half of the map is searched by non-scouting agents focused on other tasks, doing their job. The rest of the map is explored by scouts, following a greedy search algorithm. The greedy search algorithm simply finds the closest unexplored square to the scout agent, and sends the agent in that direction. Because we only update our explored map when we receive an update from the server and not when we send out a scout, if agents with the same speed happen to move to the same point, they cannot stop moving exactly on top of each other. In rare cases this leads to less efficient scouting.

3   Evaluation

We estimate that around half of the code could be recycled from last year. This includes almost all of the perception handling and processing as well as initial agent and artifact setup. Of course new percepts have been added this year and some changed, but the overall framework could be recycled from last year. Incidentally, delayed percept handling was actually one of our major problems as discussed below and we are still unsure when this error was introduced but it was probably due to our inexperience with Jason.

This year's focus on resource nodes over shops, addition of wells, as well as our own switch of strategy meant that a lot of the agent code could not be recycled.

3.1 Strengths of Our Agent Team

One of the core strengths of our solution is the versatility of the agents. While a few of our agents are bound to one role, namely assemblers, scouts, and initial destroyers, all others are dynamically allocated to the tasks they are needed for and to which they are best suited. For instance, no agents are idle at the beginning of a simulation while some resource node types are still undiscovered. Instead, all would-be gatherers take on the roles of scouts in order to efficiently discover most of the map before beginning to gather. Simultaneously, if the starting capital is sufficient to build any type of well, an appropriate number of gatherers take on the role of well builders. At the start of most simulations this means that our team starts producing points almost immediately. Furthermore, because agents are scattered around the map initially, we should discover all types of resource nodes within very few rounds. Depending on the size of the map, it is also very likely that we find the nodes closest to our desired workshop. All throughout the simulation, no specific set of agents is the well building team – gatherers and destroyers are assigned to build wells dynamically once we have sufficient money for building a new well. Builders are prioritized primarily by their *skill* and secondarily by their euclidean distance to the periphery of the map.

Another great example of agent versatility is the realization during a simulation that adequate resources have been collected, allowing gatherers to become destroyers and thus destroying enemy wells much faster and limiting the point production of the opponent. In all 7 simulations that our team won, this played a crucial role during the final stages. When nearly every agent scouts, assuming that agents scout relatively evenly due to the randomness of their paths, enemy wells are discovered within few rounds, and since so many agents are able to assist in destruction, the wells do not stand for many rounds and sometimes are not even completed. This part of the strategy could be refined more, which we discuss in the next section.

Since the majority of our agents are gatherers for most of the game, we ensure that we can gather resources evenly according to the amount of base items required for all higher tier items. Because we know locations of at least one of each type of resource node, and we collect from the ones closest to our selected workshop, an even distribution of gathered resources enables us to build higher tier items within few rounds, which in turn allows us to complete jobs shortly after the first batch of resources arrives. We assemble higher tier items in advance to be able to solve as many types of jobs as possible as soon as possible.

Finally, we decided that spending money on upgrades was not worth the cost compared to the relatively insignificant boosts to agents that they provide. While this decision was based on the figures from the example simulations, the prices during the contest were similar and thus not worthwhile. This means that we are able to afford more wells, in turn providing us more points.

3.2 Weaknesses of Our Agent Team

End Game Cutoff. During the competition it became apparent that converting gatherers to destroyers during the end game was a good strategy, especially since you gain massium by destroying an enemy well. For instance, we could not have won against SMART_JaCaMo on the Berlin map without this strategy. In that simulation, we reached the cutoff already one third into the simulation because resource nodes were located so relatively close to the storage. This gave us a long end-game where we managed to destroy more wells than would be possible with only the three original destroyers. When the simulation ended, the main storage was still 35% full. In the other simulations, it was typically even more full because the cutoff was reached later. As such, we gathered a lot more resources than we managed to utilize; a waste of effort. One solution to this would be a smaller cutoff, so that we would switch to the end game earlier but picking too small a value could make us run out of resources and thus unable to complete jobs. A better strategy would be to switch dynamically between gathering and destroying when the storage is respectively under- and overstocked.

Well Destruction. The match against TUBDAI exposed a major flaw in our strategy for destroying wells: We only use trucks to do so. What the other team had discovered was that every competition map has places that only drones can access. Only building on these spots is slower since drones are not efficient well builders, but it also makes the wells take longer to destroy as drones are not efficient destroyers either. Since we have no drone destroyers, we could never destroy TUBDAI's wells and thus they won every round against us. Even worse, if we managed to spot one of their wells, our destroyers would be rendered useless by trying over and over to find a route to the well. This latter problem is expanded upon below.

Another flaw in our well destruction strategy has to do with over centralization: We prioritize one well at a time for destruction, meaning that some destroyers may move far away from an enemy well to destroy a different one before then realizing that they have to move back again.

Well Building. The competition revealed several problems with our strategy for building wells. Firstly, it does not at all take the enemy team into account when choosing a position for the well. This meant that we might build a well right in vision of an enemy agent and have it destroyed immediately. In the worst case we might build a well right by a facility that they used. Furthermore, while our strategy of building in the periphery meant that wells might not be easily discovered by accident, it meant that they could easily be scouted by an agent with this specific purpose. Several of the other teams did this peripheral scouting, putting us at a disadvantage.

We chose to use trucks to build wells because they can do so quickly, but only once they have arrived at the location of the future well. Since trucks are the vehicles with the lowest speed, it is possibly better to pick another vehicle that can arrive faster but then spend a little longer building. Doing this also makes it easier for the enemy to destroy the well before it is fully built, because the integrity increases at a lower rate, but if they have discovered it, it will probably be destroyed either way.

When it comes to protecting wells, we do not do anything besides trying to hide them as described. It might be worth rebuilding them when they have been damaged by the enemy team. On the other hand, to do this persistently requires actively monitoring them, either constantly or periodically, to notice that they have been hurt. We deemed that the agents required for this were better allocated elsewhere. There is a compromise, however, which is probably worth doing given the time, namely to rebuild wells if you happen to notice that they are being destroyed.

Charging. We had a problem with charging on the competition maps. The logic for charging was inherited from last year and said that if an agent could not reach its target with 35% charge left, then it should charge at the nearest charging station before going to its destination. The nearest station might be in the opposite direction but this was apparently not a problem last year. We changed this logic to be that, considering only the reachable charging stations, the agent should go to the one nearest its destination. Unfortunately we still had problems with agents stranding on the Copenhagen map or going into charging loops in São Paulo when picking a destination too far away.

Delayed Responses. A major technical weakness has been a delayed response to percepts which we are still unsure of the origin of, but in all likelihood we have introduced the error somehow. No matter what, the problem means that agents will generally try to execute actions too many times because they do not immediately perceive them as successful and therefore try again. For example, the agents will try to deliver jobs twice because, despite explicitly waiting for all percepts to be processed before continuing, they think the previous delivery failed randomly. More problematically, agents might try to retrieve a number of items twice from storage leaving no room for the rest of the items. We mitigated this by only retrying retrieves after all other items had been retrieved, at which point the inventory of the agent had most likely been updated. This problem made our agents less effective than they could be as every type of agent lost a few steps occasionally due to the delayed percepts.

Route Finding. We had another technical problem that related to route finding and GraphHopper. This problem manifested itself this year where agents could not always move to named destinations but for resource nodes or exploration move to a set of coordinates instead. We use GraphHopper to, given an arbitrary point on the map, find the nearest point reachable by road. Occasionally GraphHopper would refuse to do this and despite inserted bounds the code would loop indefinitely. When this happened, the agent looking for a route would be rendered useless. This happened especially to destroyers as they constantly find random places to go to. The problem meant further that we might not build wells when we wanted to, since the task was likely given to a destroyer that was inactive. When the problem became too serious, it could be fixed by restarting the client, at the expense of having to re-explore the map and forgetting about any current jobs and item reservations. After a restart, the agents would then immediately build wells for all the accumulated massium. Furthermore, restarting made logic for tasks such as assembly more complicated as agents then had to either take the leftover items from before the restart into account or start by emptying their inventory in the main storage.

Primary Storage Choice. Our strategy of always picking the storage and workshop pair closest to each other was designed so that primary assemblers would not have to move too far back and forth, spending all their time on that instead of assembling. This simple strategy turned out to be too naive for some configurations of the maps. In unlucky cases, we would pick a pair that might have the smallest distance between them but were far away from any resource nodes or other delivery points. This likely wasted more time because gatherers would have to move further and there are more of these. A more complex criterion should be used for selecting the storage and workshop to use, preferably something that takes the placement of resource nodes into account. Doing this, however, requires postponing the choice to after scouting is done, but may turn out to be a net benefit in the end.

Jobs. Our attitude towards jobs is that there are plenty of them, so it does not matter to forgo one because another will arrive. As such, we only pursue jobs that we already have the items to complete. With the parameters in the competition this seems to be an overall good strategy, but if the items needed for jobs are not uniformly distributed but say one item is needed a lot more than the rest, we do not discover this. As such, what items we choose to assemble and store should probably be influenced by the job postings.

A real problem with the strategy is that we treat missions in the same way: we do not bother with them if we do not have the required items when they are posted. But you get a fine for not completing a mission, so this is probably too careless a strategy. We have ideas about how to both anticipate this problem and resolve it when it arrives. First, since we already have a reservation system, it might be wise to reserve a number of items purely for mission jobs, so that these can always be solved immediately when they arrive. Dropping another job because the items are reserved for a mission probably does not matter since the mission both pays in itself and we avoid the fine. Missing more jobs because of reserved items might matter though, especially since it can mean getting wells built later and thus netting fewer points in the long run, so this is a trade-off.

A second option is to reserve the items only when the mission job comes in and hope that they can be assembled in time to solve it. Furthermore, we might void other reservations to prioritize the mission. None of this was implemented due to time constraints.

Finally on the subject of jobs we turn to auction jobs. We handled these last year but in the update to the new version of the scenario and our new strategy the support was lost. As such, we completely ignore auction jobs which is both an advantage to the opponent team if they bid on one and a disadvantage for us in terms of solving more jobs. An obvious improvement to our agent team is to implement bidding on and solving auction jobs again.

Rigidness. Looking at these weaknesses we now turn to a common theme in some of them. Inspired by last year's winner we decided to divide the agents into predefined groups, each responsible for one class of things like gathering resources or assembling items. As outlined previously, some groups are dynamically managed. However, this division has still become too sharp. Agents cannot break out of their group unless explicitly asked to, as in the case of well building, and this rigidness causes situations to arise that seem silly to an observer. For instance, when a gatherer spots an enemy well it should just start destroying it, as it can be done in quite few steps. Instead, it just carries on, leaving the nearest destroyer to handle it, even though this destroyer might be on the other side of the map. Similarly, deliverers are a fixed category when there should probably be fewer of them in the beginning to prioritize gathering and more in the end to deliver more jobs. We have seen how the end game cutoff is too rigid and the distinction between gatherers and destroyers should instead be a lot more dynamic, responding to the number of items in storage compared to the demand. If we were to do things over, we would keep the overall groups but allow much more fluidity in assignments.

3.3   On the Choice of Programming Language and Frameworks

Our lack of experience with Jason meant that we had to spend some time learning the language that might have been better spent on testing and improving the strategy. Similarly, being able to recycle code from last year was both an advantage because it meant we had to write less code, but getting to know the code took some time, and, as detailed above, we encountered problems that we could not figure out how to solve.

However, Jason allowed us to easily assign agents to the groups outlined previously, write code for each of these in AgentSpeak and have the right agents perform the right actions independently of each other. This was a great benefit during development as each of us could work on a different type of agent independently, while still relying on common infrastructure, and then merge the work without any serious conflicts. The declarative nature of AgentSpeak also made a lot of the agent behaviour fairly easy to express and quite reliable.

The contract net protocol provided by CArtAgO worked really well for easily picking the best deliverers for a job. Each agent makes an estimate for how much of the job they can deliver and how fast, places a bid and is then told whether they win or not and act accordingly. Making this estimate is tricky, but the protocol itself worked without issues.

3.4   Matches

In the following we evaluate the performance of our agents in each of the four played matches. Appendix A contains visualizations of key figures for each simulation such as wells owned, jobs completed, etc.

Match 1: Akuanduba-UDESC vs. Jason-DTU. Our opponents had issues during this match, and so did we. Many were small bugs that had to be hot-fixed during the matches. For this reason, we were not able to start building wells, gathering resources, or completing jobs until quite far into the first simulation. Additionally, we had never tested on as large maps as the São Paulo map, which meant that in the third simulation, most of our agents stopped performing actions, and we were not able to fix this until after step 600 of the simulation. In general, this first match was less interesting than the later ones since both teams had issues, but once we had solved ours, we won every simulation by a fairly big margin.

Match 2: Jason-DTU vs. Smart_JaCaMo. An interesting thing about this match was that both teams had very similar strategies. In general, the idea for both teams was to gather resources to one centralized storage facility and build items at a designated workshop.

In the first simulation, both teams completed jobs at an almost identical pace. Initially, we were able to create the most wells, but Smart_JaCaMo started finding and destroying them soon after – at the same time as they built many wells of their own. For the remainder of the simulation, we were only able to destroy some of their wells, while they continued to find ours, meaning that while we were generating points, it was always at a slower pace than our opponents. When we reached 85% capacity in our designated storage facility, we were still unable to destroy their wells faster than they could build them. While the scores of each team were almost identical up to step 400, Smart_JaCaMo ended up with roughly double the score.

Our team won the second round after only being ahead in the last 10% of the simulation. There were several reasons for the success of our agents. Firstly, we gathered resources incredibly quickly. This was presumably the result of advantageous resource node locations, and it meant that we stopped gathering resources before step 400. As a result, every time Smart_JaCaMo could build wells, we destroyed them fairly quickly with our large number of destroyers.

Simultaneously, they were unable to destroy many of our wells, so once the amount started rising steadily, we generated score at an exponential pace. The final key to victory was the fact that our opponents almost stopped completing jobs around step 600, meaning that while we kept earning massium, their only source of income was destruction of our wells.

The final round on São Paulo was an easy win for our opponents. Much like in the first match, dealing with the large map meant that we were unable to build wells and complete jobs until very late in the simulation. We still gathered resources and in fact once again almost filled our storage facility, but since we did not really complete jobs until a very late stage, this was mostly in vain.

Seeing as we had very similar strategies, this matchup was very interesting. Smart_JaCaMo ended up winning the entire tournament, and we were in fact the only team to win a round against them.

Match 3: Dumping to Gather vs. Jason-DTU. This match was probably the most equal match we had. Both teams were doing great and in the end it came down to subtle differences in strategy.

In the first two rounds we successfully completed 3 to 5 times more jobs than Dumping to Gather, and therefore we acquired more massium. We used this extra massium to build wells, but while we built more wells our wells had a significantly shorter lifespan than Dumping to Gather's. They were far more effective at tracking down and destroying our wells than we were with theirs. So much so that even with us earning 3–5 times as much massium we still only won by 14% and 30% respectively. Furthermore, in round 2 we reached the 85% capacity in our storage facility. As soon as this happened there was a rapid decline in Dumping to Gather's amount of wells, which caused their score to almost stagnate, securing us the otherwise very close round.

The last round was a somewhat different story. Here, we completed jobs at a similar rate as Dumping to Gather and built roughly the same number of wells as them. Because of the much larger map none of our wells were found or destroyed before 600 steps have elapsed. This gave us a nice head start in points that Dumping to Gather could not catch up to, even though their wells doubled within the last 200 steps.

Match 4: Jason-DTU vs. TUBDAI. This match showed the most interesting strategy. TUBDAI's strategy was to build wells with their drones in places inaccessible to vehicles other than drones, which made our destroyers' job way more difficult and in fact impossible since they were all trucks. TUBDAI also had a very efficient strategy to find and destroy our wells; we always build our wells on the perimeter of the map in the hopes of these being less likely to be discovered, but TUBDAI had one drone assigned to constantly flying around the perimeter to find wells as they had presumably foreseen this strategy of well placement, which was also utilized by most teams. The combination of our inability to destroy their wells and them destroying our wells within 50 steps of completion made for a big loss for us. In all 3 rounds they had an exponential growth in score, while we only had small upticks.

We did however seem to be more effective than them in completing jobs (specifically in rounds 2 and 3), which displays the strength of our implementation with regards to job execution. Also, we were able to score points in all rounds.

4 Conclusion

We have provided a brief description of the multi-agent system that the Jason-DTU team developed for the Multi-Agent Programming Contest 2018. We reused the framework that we made in Jason as part of our 2017 system with the agents modified to suit the new scenario. Using Jason and CArtAgO we could take advantage of the contract net protocol to coordinate our agents, and the declarative nature of AgentSpeak made the agent behavior easy to express and to make reliable. To facilitate coordination we implemented groups that agents dynamically could enter and leave depending on the current situation, a reservation system for which agents could reserve required resources before retrieving them, and strategic phases for directing the team in decentralized manner.

The strengths of our system include the flexible use of agents, as agents are not locked to a specific purpose for the entirety of a match simulation but can change group accordingly to the current situation and phase of the strategy, allowing agents to be responsive to changes in the environment.

We have also identified key weaknesses in our agent system, in particular regarding which agents we allowed to be used for destroying wells. In our match against TUBDAI the opposing team built wells at locations only accessible to drones which we did not use for destroying wells. Our team was efficient at clearing missions and building wells but ultimately could not deal with the opposing strategy.

Overall our team performed very well though and we won some matches by either a fairly big margin or closely, ending up at a third place in the contest.

Acknowledgements. Thanks to Oliver Fleckenstein and Helge Hatteland for insights based on the Jason-DTU team last year.

A   Team Overview: Short Answers

A.1   Participants and Their Background

What was your motivation to participate in the contest? To work on implementing a multi-agent system capable of competing in a realistic, albeit simulated, scenario.

What is the history of your group? (course project, thesis, ...) The group is a mix of computer scientists and students working on a special course.

What is your field of research? Which work therein is related? We are from the Department of Applied Mathematics and Computer Science at the Technical University of Denmark (DTU). We are part of AlgoLoG, the Algorithms, Logic and Graphs section, which is responsible for the Artificial Intelligence and Algorithms study line of the MSc in Computer Science and Engineering programme.

A.2   Development

How much time did you invest in the contest for programming vs. other tasks (for example organization)? Most of the time went into programming and debugging. The desired strategy was settled quickly and we had little time for testing in the end.

creating vs. optimizing your agents? We estimate an 80–20% split between creating and optimizing.

How many lines of code did you produce for your final agent team? 5645 lines of Java code and 657 lines of AgentSpeak. We note that some of the code was reused from last year.

How many people were involved and to which degree? Five people were involved with three of them doing most of the work and all of the implementation.

When did you start working on your agents? We started working on the implementation of our agents September 3, 2018 having started a week earlier to get the new scenario running.

A.3   System Details

How do your agents work together? (coordination, information sharing, ...) Designated responsibilities and information sharing. Occasional centrally determined designation of other responsibilities.

What are critical components of your team? Agents are split into 4 primary and mostly static groups: resource gatherers, well destroyers, scouts, and item assemblers.

Can your agents change their behavior during runtime? If so, what triggers the changes? Accumulating enough massium triggers a resource gatherer or destroyer agent to become a well builder instead. Discovering an enemy well makes destroyer agents target the well instead of scouting. When the main storage is 85% full, resource gatherers become destroyer agents instead. When one of each type of resource node is found, initial scouts take on other responsibilities.

Did you have to make changes to the team (e.g. fix critical bugs) during the contest? Yes, our code did not work at all for the beginning of the first match because the simulation was named differently than during testing causing a parsing error.

How do you organize your agents? Do you use e.g. hierarchies? Is your organization implicit or explicit? They are organized in explicit groups and may be occasionally moved from one group to another and back again. The groups are not subordinated to each other.

Is most of your agents' behavior emergent on an individual or team level? The behavior of the agents is primarily designed rather than emergent, both at an individual and team level.

If your agents perform some planning, how many steps do they plan ahead? No planning is performed.

If you have a perceive-think-act cycle, how is it synchronized with the server? After an agent performs an action it waits for a step event. We collect every percept in each round and only then announce the step so the agents start thinking and acting based on the new percepts.

How did you go about debugging your system? Debugging was done very primitively using print statements.

Which operating system did you use, and is your team portable to other operating systems? We used macOS and Linux (Ubuntu and Fedora) during development and ran the system on Windows for the competition.

What hardware did you use to run your agent team? (RAM, CPU, disk space, multiple computers, any other notable requirements) For the contest we used a single computer with the 10-core Intel Core i9-7900X, Corsair DDR4 PC2666 128GB RAM and Samsung 960 PRO 2TB M.2 PCIe SSD. We could have used a much less powerful computer if necessary.

A.4   Scenario and Strategy

What is the main strategy of your agent team? Designate different responsibilities to each group of agents, then collect needed resources, build and store items, and deliver jobs in a parallel, pipeline fashion with intermittent well building.

How do your agents decide which jobs to complete? If we currently have the needed items in storage, we reserve them and attempt the job.

Do you have different strategies for the different roles? Indirectly, as we impose our own groups with distinct responsibilities on subsets of the agents. We assign agents to subsets depending on their roles. Some subsets are managed dynamically.

Do your agents form ad-hoc teams to complete a task? No. The group of well builders is managed in an ad-hoc fashion but there is no in-group coordination. Item assemblers are always present to assist in assembly and thus do not require any coordination.

How do your agents decide when and where to build wells? When enough massium is available to build any type of well, we pick the type that we deem most effective and designate a free resource gatherer or destroyer truck to build it at the nearest peripheral point.

If your agents accumulated a lot of currency, why did they not spend it immediately? The route-finding logic for the well builders was prone to loop, rendering an agent useless but this was not detected by the other agents, so no one else was designated to build the well instead. After restarting the system, we would immediately build a lot of wells.

A.5   Discussion

What did you learn from participating in the contest? How to implement a multi-agent system in Jason. The importance of testing on different maps with various configurations because it is easy to make assumptions that end up not holding.

What are the strong and weak points of your team? Once we get going we are efficient at collecting needed resources and building up a storage of various items. Our team structure is relatively static making us less efficient in some cases. Some of our logic causes endless iterations of useless series of actions or no action at all, causing several agents to be stuck.

How viable were your chosen programming language, methodology, tools, and algorithms? Working with Jason and CArtAgO had benefits with regards to implementing decentralized decision making and reusing logic for different agent groups. However, our limited experience with these tools caused us to use them less efficiently than we would have liked. Our general methodology seems to provide consistently good results unless the opponent is able to specifically target our well building strategy.

Did you encounter new problems during the contest? Yes, we encountered a parsing problem right at the beginning and problems with our route finding going into infinite loops requiring us to restart those agents. We also experienced problems when no resource nodes could be perceived initially. Some faults in agent logic were exposed on the São Paulo map.

Did playing against other agent teams bring about new insights on your own agents? Yes, in particular it revealed situations where more fluidity in assigned responsibility would be beneficial. It also exposed our agents' obliviousness to the positions of agents from the other team in many cases.

What would you improve if you wanted to participate in the same contest a week from now (or next year)? Fix the bug where some percepts were sometimes delayed a round making us less efficient. We would make the responsibilities less rigid, for instance by dynamically switching resource gatherers into well destroyers and vice versa depending on demand. Not build wells near enemy agents and not build them in spots where they were repeatedly detected, like when an enemy drone scouts the periphery where we built all our wells. Allow other roles than trucks to build and destroy wells.

Which aspect of your team cost you the most time? Implementing the various strategies for the different responsibility groups.

Why did your team perform as it did? Why did the other teams perform better/worse than you did? Our ability to start generating points almost immediately and our group distribution of agents was efficient. Destroying wells during the endgame caused us to dominate some otherwise very close games. One team was able to counter our well building strategy by scouting the periphery of the maps all the time and almost immediately destroying our wells.

A.6   The Future of the MAPC

What can be improved regarding the contest for next year? We would like the map to be simpler, so that less time can be spent dealing with navigation. All reachable locations should be reachable by all roles unless explicitly specified.

What kind of scenario would you like to play next? What kind of features should the new scenario have? We suggest making the efficiency of well nodes depend on the location, for example making hard to reach places only support low efficiency well nodes. That way there can be a trade-off between making hard to destroy but inefficient well nodes vs easy to destroy but efficient well nodes.

Should the teams be allowed to make changes to their agents during the contest (even based on opponent agent behavior observed in earlier matches)? If yes, should only some changes be legal and which ones (e.g. bugfixes), and how to decide a change's classification? If no, should we ensure that no changes are made and how? We think bug fixes should be allowed as getting everything tested and working up-front can be difficult. Classification is inherently difficult, but we believe at least that changes based on the other team's behaviour should not be allowed. Strict guidelines should be made, although they are hard to uphold, and in the end the team's conscience has to guide their decisions on changes.

Do you have ideas to reduce the impact of unforeseen strategies (e.g., playing a second leg after some time)? It did seem like a shame that you could gain a big advantage this year by placing wells where only drones could reach them. A less intricate map design would diminish the impact of such strategies. The disadvantage with a second leg however is that the results will likely depend a lot on who has more time available to prepare for it (Figs. 1, 2, 3, 4, 5, 6, 7, 8, 9, 10, 11 and 12).

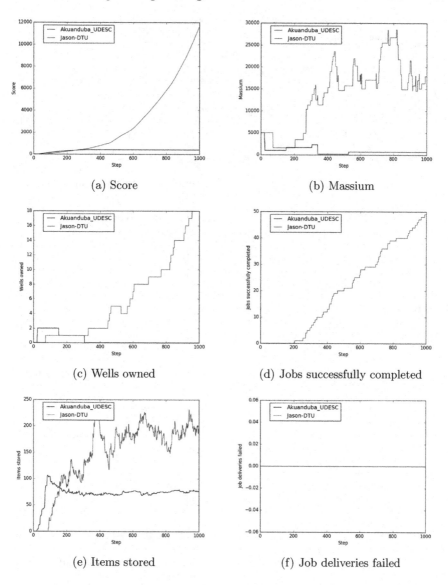

(a) Score

(b) Massium

(c) Wells owned

(d) Jobs successfully completed

(e) Items stored

(f) Job deliveries failed

Fig. 1. Simulation 1 – Akuanduba-UDESC vs. Jason-DTU

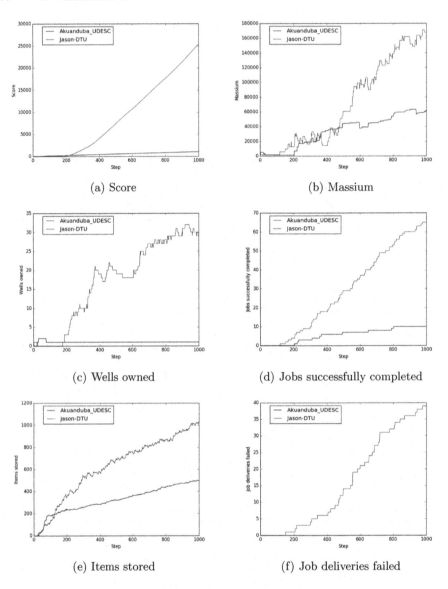

(a) Score

(b) Massium

(c) Wells owned

(d) Jobs successfully completed

(e) Items stored

(f) Job deliveries failed

Fig. 2. Simulation 2 – Akuanduba-UDESC vs. Jason-DTU

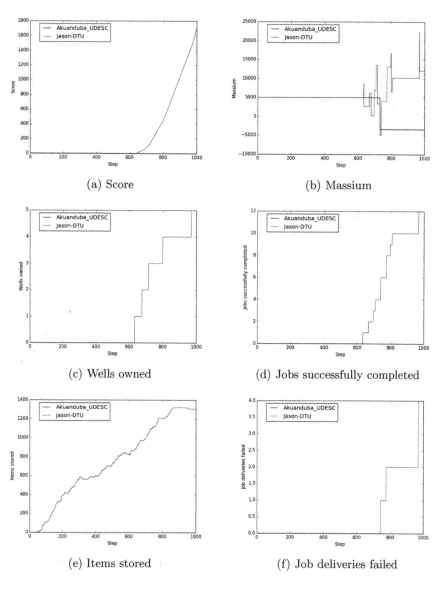

(a) Score

(b) Massium

(c) Wells owned

(d) Jobs successfully completed

(e) Items stored

(f) Job deliveries failed

Fig. 3. Simulation 3 – Akuanduba-UDESC vs. Jason-DTU

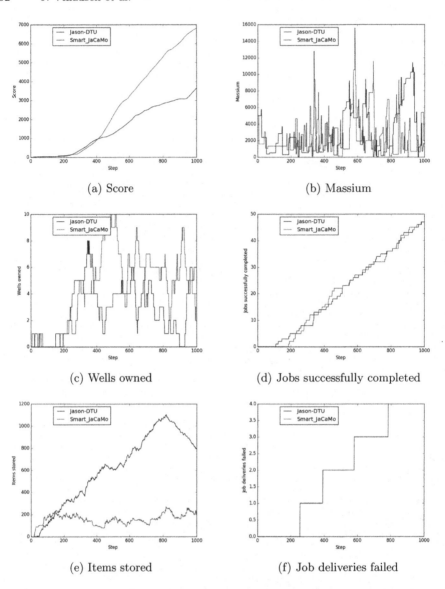

(a) Score

(b) Massium

(c) Wells owned

(d) Jobs successfully completed

(e) Items stored

(f) Job deliveries failed

Fig. 4. Simulation 1 – Jason-DTU vs. Smart_JaCaMo

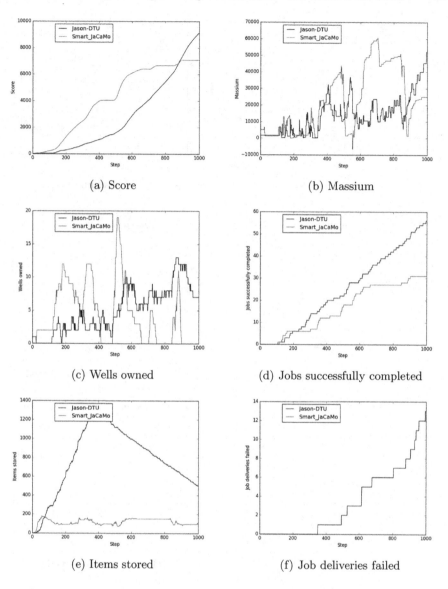

(a) Score

(b) Massium

(c) Wells owned

(d) Jobs successfully completed

(e) Items stored

(f) Job deliveries failed

Fig. 5. Simulation 2 – Jason-DTU vs. Smart_JaCaMo

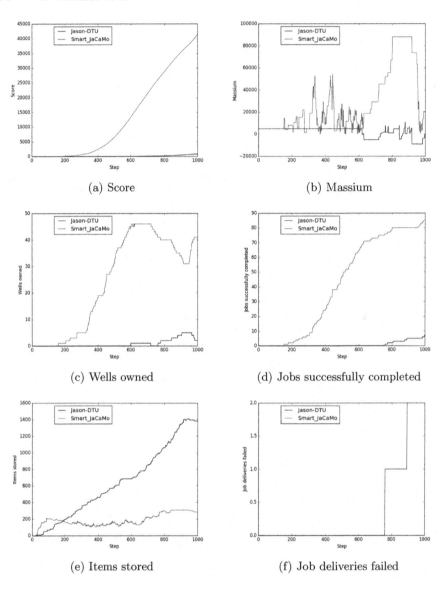

(a) Score

(b) Massium

(c) Wells owned

(d) Jobs successfully completed

(e) Items stored

(f) Job deliveries failed

Fig. 6. Simulation 3 – Jason-DTU vs. Smart_JaCaMo

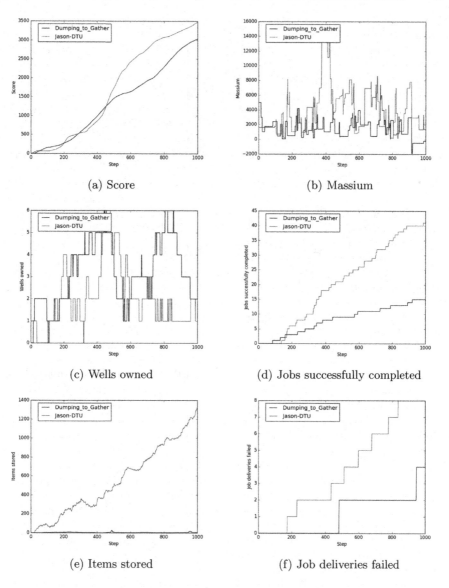

(a) Score

(b) Massium

(c) Wells owned

(d) Jobs successfully completed

(e) Items stored

(f) Job deliveries failed

Fig. 7. Simulation 1 – Dumping to Gather vs. Jason-DTU

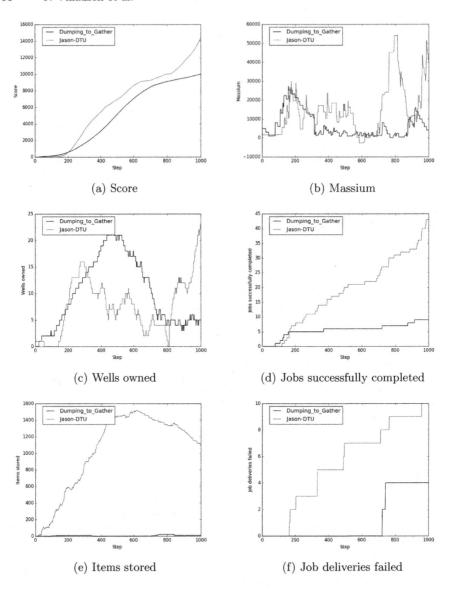

(a) Score

(b) Massium

(c) Wells owned

(d) Jobs successfully completed

(e) Items stored

(f) Job deliveries failed

Fig. 8. Simulation 2 – Dumping to Gather vs. Jason-DTU

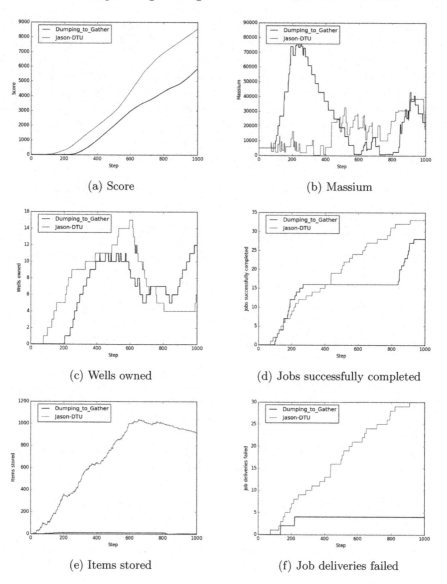

(a) Score

(b) Massium

(c) Wells owned

(d) Jobs successfully completed

(e) Items stored

(f) Job deliveries failed

Fig. 9. Simulation 3 – Dumping to Gather vs. Jason-DTU

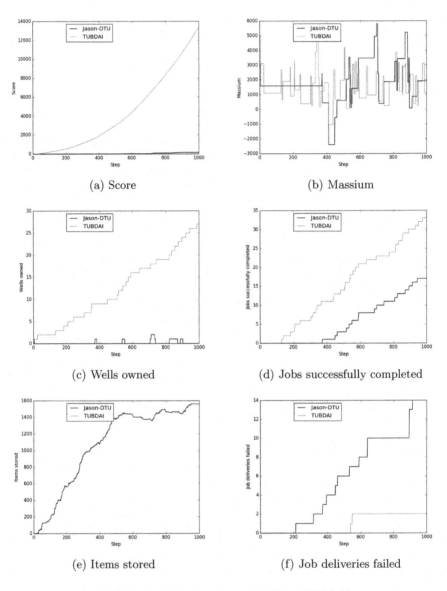

(a) Score

(b) Massium

(c) Wells owned

(d) Jobs successfully completed

(e) Items stored

(f) Job deliveries failed

Fig. 10. Simulation 1 – Jason-DTU vs. TUBDAI

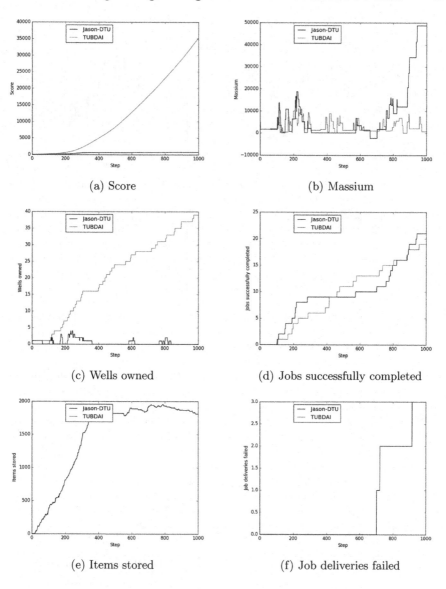

(a) Score

(b) Massium

(c) Wells owned

(d) Jobs successfully completed

(e) Items stored

(f) Job deliveries failed

Fig. 11. Simulation 2 – Jason-DTU vs. TUBDAI

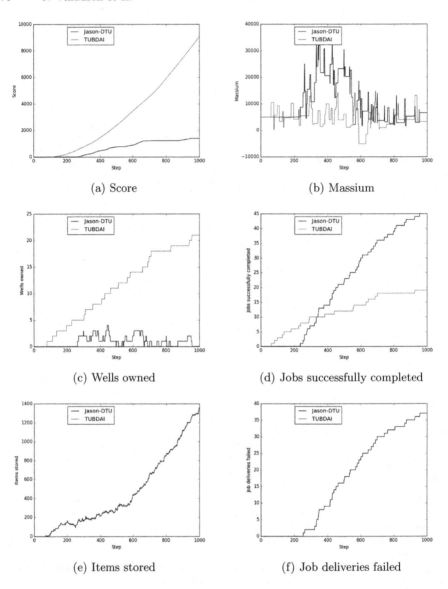

(a) Score

(b) Massium

(c) Wells owned

(d) Jobs successfully completed

(e) Items stored

(f) Job deliveries failed

Fig. 12. Simulation 3 – Jason-DTU vs. TUBDAI

References

1. Bordini, R.H., Hübner, J.F., Wooldridge, M.: Programming Multi-agent Systems in AgentSpeak Using Jason. Wiley, Hoboken (2007)
2. Ricci, A., Piunti, M., Viroli, M.: Environment programming in multi-agent systems: an artifact-based perspective. Auton. Agents Multi-Agent Syst. **23**(2), 158–192 (2011)
3. Boss, N.S., Jensen, A.S., Villadsen, J.: Building multi-agent systems using Jason. Ann. Math. Artif. Intell. **59**, 373–388 (2010)
4. Vester, S., Boss, N.S., Jensen, A.S., Villadsen, J.: Improving multi-agent systems using Jason. Ann. Math. Artif. Intell. **61**, 297–307 (2011)
5. Ettienne, M.B., Vester, S., Villadsen, J.: Implementing a multi-agent system in python with an auction-based agreement approach. In: Dennis, L., Boissier, O., Bordini, R.H. (eds.) ProMAS 2011. LNCS (LNAI), vol. 7217, pp. 185–196. Springer, Heidelberg (2012). https://doi.org/10.1007/978-3-642-31915-0_11
6. Villadsen, J., Jensen, A.S., Ettienne, M.B., Vester, S., Andersen, K.B., Frøsig, A.: Reimplementing a multi-agent system in python. In: Dastani, M., Hübner, J.F., Logan, B. (eds.) ProMAS 2012. LNCS, vol. 7837, pp. 205–216. Springer, Heidelberg (2013). https://doi.org/10.1007/978-3-642-38700-5_13
7. Villadsen, J., Jensen, A.S., Christensen, N.C., Hess, A.V., Johnsen, J.B., Woller, Ø.G., Ørum, P.B.: Engineering a multi-agent system in GOAL. In: Cossentino, M., El Fallah Seghrouchni, A., Winikoff, M. (eds.) EMAS 2013. LNCS (LNAI), vol. 8245, pp. 329–338. Springer, Heidelberg (2013). https://doi.org/10.1007/978-3-642-45343-4_18
8. Villadsen, J., From, A.H., Jacobi, S., Larsen, N.N.: Multi-agent programming contest 2016 – the python-DTU team. Int. J. Agent-Oriented Softw. Eng. **6**(1), 86–100 (2018)
9. Villadsen, J., Fleckenstein, O., Hatteland, H., Larsen, J.B.: Engineering a multi-agent system in Jason and CArtAgO. Ann. Math. Artif. Intell. **84**, 57–74 (2018)

SMART–JaCaMo: An Organisation-Based Team for the Multi-Agent Programming Contest

Tabajara Krausburg[1]([✉]), Rafael Cauê Cardoso[2], Juliana Damasio[1],
Vitor Peres[1], Giovani P. Farias[1], Débora Cristina Engelmann[1],
Jomi Fred Hübner[3], and Rafael H. Bordini[1]

[1] School of Technology, PUCRS, Porto Alegre, Brazil
{tabajara.rodrigues,juliana.damasio,vitor.peres,
debora.engelmann}@edu.pucrs.br,
giovani.farias@acad.pucrs.br, rafael.bordini@pucrs.br
[2] University of Liverpool, Liverpool, UK
rafael.cardoso@liverpool.ac.uk
[3] Federal University of Santa Catarina, Florianópolis, Brazil
jomi.hubner@ufsc.br

Abstract. The Multi-Agent Programming Contest in 2018 expanded upon the Agents in the City scenario used in the 2016 and 2017 editions of the contest. In this scenario two teams compete to score points by building and attacking wells using realistic city maps from OpenStreetMap. Wells are the main addition to the new version of the scenario; they cost money to build and generate score overtime but can be dismantled by agents from the other team. This, along with other additions, made it a significantly more complex scenario than before. In this paper, we describe the strategies used by our team, highlighting our adaptations and new additions from our participation in the previous years. We have fully explored the use of all three programming dimensions (agent, environment, and organisation) available in JaCaMo, the multi-agent system development platform that we used to implement our team. Our agents were able to dynamically switch between organisational roles, allowing them to promptly respond to changes in the environment and different opponent strategies. We were the highest-scoring team in the contest and our multi-agent system turned out to be stable and robust in solving the difficult problems posed by the contest scenario.

Keywords: Multi-Agent Programming Contest · Role-based multi-agent systems · Agents in the City · JaCaMo

This study was financed in part by the Coordenação de Aperfeiçoamento de Pessoal de Nível Superior – Brasil (CAPES) – Finance Code 001.

T. Ahlbrecht et al. (Eds.): MAPC 2018, LNAI 11957, pp. 72–100, 2019.
https://doi.org/10.1007/978-3-030-37959-9_4

1   Introduction

The Multi-Agent Programming Contest (MAPC) started in 2005 as an annual international event. It was created by Dix and Mehdi Dastani [2]. Year after year, there is an ongoing effort promoted by the contest organisers to make challenging competition in complex scenarios. This year was the third edition of the "Agents in the City" scenario introduced in 2016 [1]. That scenario consists of two teams playing against each other in a map of real city. Each team has a number of vehicle agents (drones, cars, trucks, and motorcycles) moving through the streets of the map. The contest goal is to build and keep as many wells as possible to score more points. In order to build wells, a team needs to complete jobs assembling and delivering items.

Some of the main changes in relation to MAPC 2017 are as follows. The number of agents per team increased from 28 to 34 agents. Regarding the auction jobs, a new rule was added whereby the auction time (and the job ending step) are increased by one every time a team posts a new bid at the last step of the auction phase. Agents can buy upgrades on speed, load (carrying capacity), battery, vision, and skill. A team can build wells for generating scores; now scores are used to determine the winner of a round. Items are not bought, base items can be gathered with **gather** actions and compound item are assembled in *workshops*. This year's competition scenario has three city maps: Copenhagen, Berlin, and São Paulo. The maps were released 3 days before the contest began.

Our team has been participating in the MAPC [10,11] since 2016. We have adapted our code from previous years using the JaCaMo programming platform [5]. This year, we further explored other aspects of Jason and $\mathcal{M}$OISE. The source code for our MAPC 2018 team is available for download at https://github.com/smart-pucrs/mapc2018-pucrs.

This paper is structured as follows: Sect. 2 introduces the JaCaMo platform and some important architectural elements that we used to develop our strategies. Section 3 we explain some of the specialist behaviour built into our agents. Section 4 provides a detailed description of our strategy. In Sect. 5 we analyse our team against the main opponents, and in Sect. 6 we answer the questions posed by the contest organisers. Finally, we make final remarks and discuss future work in Sect. 7.

2   Software Architecture

Our team was developed using the JaCaMo[1] multi-agent programming framework [5], which combines three different technologies, each focused on a different level of abstraction: agents, environment, and organisation. We used JaCaMo in the past two contests that our team participated [10,11], but in this edition of the contest we made better use of organisation concepts, such as roles and groups, which had not been used previously.

---

[1] http://jacamo.sourceforge.net/.

2.1   Jason

Jason [6] is an agent-oriented programming language that implements and extends AgentSpeak(L) [15]. Agents in Jason are based on the Belief Desire Intention (BDI) model [7,16], representing the information, motivational, and deliberative states of the agent.

A Jason agent is an entity composed of a set of beliefs (the agent's knowledge about the world), a set of goals (tasks that the agent wants to achieve), a set of intentions (what the agent is committed to doing), and a set of plans (courses of action that are triggered by events). Events include changes in the agent's belief base, and the addition or removal of goals.

Modules. We first started using Jason modules in our 2017 team [10]. Modules provide a mechanism to separate units of code, encouraging code reusability and maintaining the agent's mental state organised [12]. These modules may contain beliefs, goals, and plans, all of which are prefixed with the namespace of the module (e.g., to call the `buy_well` plan from outside of the `build` module, we use `+!build::buy_well`). The beliefs that come from the environment are kept on the default module loaded by Jason. This approach allows us to manage the agent's beliefs of particular modules, for example, when advancing to the next simulation round we need to remove/reset all beliefs in some of the modules.

We also used modules to help agents decide when they are allowed to change their intentions. In our code, a goal within a module represents the agent's commitment to a particular behaviour. For instance, consider an agent that is committed to building a well. It takes several simulation steps to finish building a well; at each step, the agent performs an action `build` that increases the well integrity. This procedure is repeated until the well's maximum integrity is reached. In a step before the well is completely built, the agent receives a new perception from the environment indicating that the team has enough `massium` (monetary unit used in the simulation) to build a new well. This agent is able to detect that it is already committed to a goal from the build module and should not change its intention to build a new well whilst it has not finished the previous one.

Meta-events. Jason meta-events are events related to goal states; each goal state transition triggers a meta-event in Jason. The general idea comes from goal lifecycles as put forward in [8], where each goal type is represented by a *state-machine* indicating the possible state transitions for goals of that type. A meta-event carries the current state of the goal in its *annotation*. The possible states of a goal in a Jason agent are: `failed`, `finished`, `resumed`, `started`, and `suspended`. For instance, an agent is executing a plan to go to some place, and then its battery gets nearly depleted. The agent suspends its current goal and starts a new intention to charge its battery. In this example, a meta-event is generated for the goal to move somewhere as it transitions from state `started` to state `suspended`, and such meta-event can trigger the adoption of new goals or the resumption of previous ones.

2.2   CArtAgO

CArtAgO [17] is based on the A&A (Agents and Artifacts) model [14]. In this model, the environment is represented as workspaces where agents and artefacts (entities that provide services to the agents) are situated. An agent that uses the *focus* action to focus on an artefact receives its *observable properties* as perceptions and is able to perform *operations* (i.e., actions) made available by that artefact.

Interaction with the Environment. In the MAPC, the environment is implemented by the server, so we do not program it directly. Instead, JSON messages are exchanged between the server and the clients (teams) via standard TCP socket communication. Although it is possible to create a direct communication with the server using their protocol, there is a standard environment interface available called EISMASSim [4] that works in the client side and abstracts much of the parsing and connecting procedures that would otherwise be necessary.

Our agents still need a way of interacting with the server to receive perceptions and to send actions in each simulation step. We do so through a dedicated environment interaction artefact for each agent, called `EISArtifact` [10,11]. This artefact keeps the observable properties updated with the newest values from each simulation step, but also filters out any perceptions that our agents do not use (such as *dumps*, or *route*), to avoid overloading the belief base of the agent.

Besides these features, the `EISArtifact` of each agent is also responsible for translating (by instantiating the `Translator` class) EISMASSim perceptions to Jason literals that are then added as observable properties, and translating Jason action literals to EISMASim actions. The environment artefact also supports on-the-fly routing (by instantiating the `MapHelper` class) via the use of the GraphHopper API[2]. This is the same route planner that is used by the server; we also use it locally so we do not have to spend an action to calculate extra routes to be able to reason about them.

Sharing Team Information. Although most of the information is decentralised, via each agent's environment artefact, there are some situations where the agents may want to share some information with the rest of the team. For example, the locations of enemy wells are not commonly known, and enemy wells are only discovered once they are within an agent's vision radius. An agent sends the information that it wants to share with the team to the `TeamArtifact`, which is focused by all agents in the team.

Besides the position of enemy wells, our agents also use this artefact to share the location of resource nodes, which are not initially known when the simulation starts. The team keeps several data structures (these data structures still have to be manually updated by each agent) that are used to aid in decision making, most

---

[2] https://www.graphhopper.com/.

notably: *desired bases* is a priority list for base items (resources) that are most often needed in the manufacturing of assembled items; and *desired compounds* is a priority list for assembled items that are most often required for job deliveries. These two priority lists are further discussed in Sect. 4.8.

Task Allocation Artefacts. As in [10,11], we continue to use the Contract Net Protocol (CNP) [18], a decentralised task allocation protocol, for allocating job tasks to our agents. As before, our implementation is based on the CNP artefact available in CArtAgO's source code. The main difference from our previous implementation is that this year we also use CNP to allocate delivery tasks, where multiple agents can contribute to the partial delivery of a job.

2.3 Moise

MOISE [13] is a language for the specification of Multi-Agent System (MAS) organisations, with support for organisation-based reasoning at the agent level. The specification is done via an XML file containing three different specifications: structural, functional, and normative. In this edition of the MAPC, we made explicit use of the first two specifications, and implicitly used organisation obedient agents at the normative level.

In the structural specification we have defined all possible roles within the organisation, but groups are created dynamically at runtime. As for the functional specification, our team dynamically instantiates a coordination scheme (an structured set of goals) to aid in the manufacturing of assembled items (i.e., complex items that require different types of resources and/or other items and/or multiple types of vehicles).

Roles, Groups, and Schemes. MOISE allows agents to be part of an organisation by playing specific roles and, by doing so, they become responsible for some particular goals in the overall process. One of the great advantages of using a MOISE organisation is that it becomes very easy to make agents change roles to adapt their behaviour accordingly. Our team had the following roles available:

Gatherer: gathers base items from resource nodes.
Builder: builds wells and, if free, helps others roles to assemble items.
Super Builder: focuses only in building wells.
Explorer: explores the map searching for resource nodes and opponent wells.
Drone Explorer: used by each of the four drones to search for resource nodes and opposing wells within a quadrant of the map.
Super Explorer: focus on searching and attacking opposing wells, upgrading the skill whenever possible.
Delivery: delivers partial/full jobs by collecting stocked items from storage and delivering them to the job's target storage.
Assembler: assembles items.
Assistant: gives assistance to the assembler agent by providing items and/or the vehicle's tool.

Attacker: dismantles wells that belong to the opponent team.

These roles are part of a general group called JaCaMo_Team. Also, we define two types of groups. The first one informs the agents which role that each teammate has adopted. The second group is created at runtime for assembling items, agents that won the tasks for assembling the compounded item adopt the role of *assistant* or *assembler*. Only one agent can commit to being assembler for a specific task, the others will be assistants. We created a scheme to coordinate agents during complex jobs that require items to be assembled. Figure 1 shows the scheme for the assembly of items. A scheme has a set of associated missions and each mission has a set of goals. We had three missions: `mretrieve` with a goal to retrieve items; `massemble` with a goal to assemble and a goal to deliver items; and `massist` with a goal to assist in assemble and a goal to stop assisting. This is a key feature of our team, so we cover some aspects of how the agents are allocated to missions and choose their roles in Sect. 4.

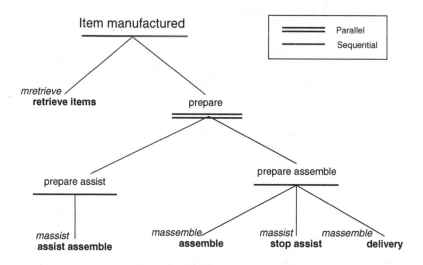

Fig. 1. Assembling scheme.

3   Programming Agent Behaviour

Here we describe the various types of behaviour that our agents display in the simulation. We use the term "behaviour" to denote a particular course of actions for simple tasks (in general, a behaviour does not depend on sophisticated reasoning about the environment).

3.1 Exploring

Our exploration process is composed of two phases, and we choose only drone agents to be responsible for this task. First, we divide the map into four quadrants; each of the four drones is responsible for exploring only one quadrant. As an example of how the quadrant exploration takes place, let us consider the fourth quadrant of a map. We draw concentric rectangles (see shaded area in Fig. 2) from the centre of the quadrant. The exploration starts from the inner rectangle and moves on to the outer ones. Considering the drone's vision skill we are able to calculate how many turns are necessary to explore the entire quadrant (i.e., how many such rectangles will be used). To do so, we only have to move the drone along the diagonal, using its vision skill range.

Fig. 2. Exploration model for the fourth quadrant on the map of São Paulo.

After traversing the entire quadrant, only two drones stay for the second phase, in which they must traverse the entire map. In this exploration, they only go through the map boundaries. Beginning from the southeast and northwest edges of the map, one goes in clockwise direction and the other goes in anticlockwise direction. The remaining two drones move on to support assembling items instead.

3.2 Build

Right after receiving the map perceptions, our builder agents perform an evaluation of the available well types to rank them according to some criteria. Our evaluation takes into account the well's prices (`massium` cost) and the number of scores per step that a well type generates (i.e., its efficiency). That rank is stored in the agent's belief base, lowest values indicating better cost-benefit ratios. When enough `massium` is available to build wells, builders always choose the best cost-benefit well type it can afford at that moment. Then it sends action `buy` followed by action `build`. It continues executing the `build` action until the well reaches its maximum integrity.

3.3 Attack

Our attacking behaviour is rather simple: it consist in attacking the adversarial well until its integrity reaches zero (i.e., the well is destroyed). Before starting an attack, the attacker must go to the well location in order to send the action `dismantle`. Which well an agent will choose to attack depends on our strategy, which is explained in Sect. 4.7. It is important to note that our attacking behaviour does not allow our agents to attack wells built by our own team.

3.4 Defence

We did not implement any defence behaviour into our agents. We followed that approach because we do not know when a well would be attacked, and letting an agent protect our wells could result in wasted simulation steps. Also, protecting a well could result in losing one agent for the rest of the match (if a defending and a attacking agent have the same skill level, they could be stuck defending/attacking a well until the match ends).

3.5 Gather

Agents that use the gather behaviour are responsible for collecting resources, that is, base items that are required to assemble more complex ones. These resources can be gathered by executing the `gather` action in a resource node facility. The gathering behaviour specifies that an agent gathers the resource until its load (carrying capacity) is full.

3.6 Assemble

To assemble an item, an agent has to execute the `assemble` action in a *workshop* facility, and unless that agent covers all of the prerequisites (is carrying all necessary base and assembled items, and is the only type of vehicle required to build the item), it will also need the help of other agents that can contribute by executing the `assist assemble` action. The assemble behaviour includes these two actions, which are only executed when the organisation's coordination scheme determines, to ensure that all participating agents are in the same location and executing their actions in the same simulation step.

Moreover, this behaviour includes a plan for handling failures. Since all agents have a random 1% chance to fail any action, if an agent fails an assemble (or assist assemble) action, then the item will not be successfully assembled. The failure handling plan ensures that the agent tries it again in the next simulation step.

3.7 Delivery

An agent that needs to deliver items to complete a job (either partially or entirely) starts by moving to the `storage` facility that contains the items that it has committed itself to deliver for that job. Should the agent be carrying any other items not related to the job, it will first store them away. This could occur for two reasons: (i) the agent was gathering items; or (ii) the agent was delivering a job that was performed first by the other team. After retrieving all necessary items, the agent moves to the specific storage that was requested in the job description and then performs the `deliver job` action.

4 Team Strategies

Here we describe the strategy that our agents adopted in the contest. A strategy is a set of rules that guide the decision-making process of our team in one particular aspect of the scenario. Usually, a strategy makes use of one or more of the types of behaviour presented in the previous section.

It is important that the reader bears in mind that our agents keep changing intentions and roles continuously, in order to respond to changes in the environment. However, not every change is allowed. Some roles specify to agents what other roles they are allowed to adopt and under which circumstances (defined by the behaviour modules). For instance, a builder is not allowed to change to any role if it is executing plans from the *build behaviour module* (i.e., building a well). After doing everything needed, the agents always tend to return to their original roles (i.e., the ones determined before the match started). That intuition guides how all our strategies are designed.

4.1 Reasoning Engine

In order to properly develop agent behaviour and strategies, we need to first define how they reason about their perceptions of the environment. This is a key part of our team of agents; without it, we would be stuck in solving bugs when adding any new behaviour or strategy. Here, we will go deeply into the three fundamental parts of each reasoning cycle carried out by agents.

Reconsidering Intentions. Any BDI agent should be able to reason about the environment and change its current intention, if needed. However, sometimes it is not trivial to implement such feature. In our team, we use Jason `internal actions` to drop agent's desires and intentions. When a new intention appears (e.g., due to environment changes) the past intentions that aim to send an action to the contest server should be dropped. To enable this, we drop every desire and intention that has a goal of sending an action to the server. After all those intentions are dropped, the agent starts to reason about which new action should be sent to the server.

There is a little problem related to this reconsideration: when a new intention appears but the past one has already sent an action to the server. In this case, before dropping the old intention, we need to wait for the agent's belief base update following perception the environment. If the agent does not do so, the new intention will start to reason about outdated beliefs, and will potentially choose a bad action to send to the server. Moreover, old intentions continue consuming agent's computing resources and may affect other coordination artefacts (e.g., `TeamArtifact`). Consider the example of an agent at `storage0` that has just stored an item. Its current intention decides to go gather; so it chooses an action `goto` and send it to the server. However, this agent is selected to assist another agent and it must retrieve an item at `storage0`. This new intention wants every other intention to be dropped and it will select an action to retrieve the desired item. At the next step, the agent is not at `storage0` because the old intention has sent a `goto` action, consequently, the action for retrieving an item will fail. This is why an intention can only start reasoning at the current step before an action has been sent or after a new step perception.

Access Tokens for Intentions. Changing intentions is not as simple as it seems. Some intentions should not be immediately dropped by any other intention; they should finish a set of particular actions before being dropped. Consider again the previous example of an agent aiming to store an item at `storage0`. It has just sent its action to store the item and is about to update the `TeamArtifact` with this information. However, a enemy well is discovered by some teammate and it starts the process of reconsidering its intentions. If the old intention (the one that has just stored the item) is dropped, the `TeamArtifact` will not be updated with the new stock quantity. On the other hand, if it is not dropped, it will end up sending another action to the server in the next step. Here, we were caught on a difficult situation; how can an agent decide the appropriate time to drop an intention?

To solve this problem, we use a strategy based on *access token*. Each intention will receive a token, and every time a new intention emerges trying to send an action to the server, it may revoke all valid tokens. In this case, only the new intention will be able to send actions. The old intentions will continue performing their goals; however, when trying to send an action to the server, they will perceive that their access token has been revoked. In the light of this information, all intentions that possess invalid tokens will eventually drop themselves without sending any further action to the server until then. This was our apparently successful attempt to solve such a difficult problem.

Waiting for Help Requests. The contest domain requires collaborative action (e.g., to assemble items); in order to cope with that, agents need to coordinate their actions at a given simulation step in order to work towards the same goal. When in need of help (e.g., an assembler agent requiring assistance), agents will send "requests for help" and when receiving one such request, an agent might need to change the action it has selected to execute. This raises an interesting problem: given a particular step, until when an agent should wait for a help request before sending its chosen action to the server[3].

For that purpose, our agents choose an action based on the environment changes at the current step. However, it does not send its action, it only keeps a belief stating which action it is. Then, it informs the other agents that its action has been chosen. When all agents choose their actions and no assistance is required, they send their actions to the server. If a help request arrives, an agent can change its action commitment in order to help another agent. It chooses its new action based on the request and immediately sends it to the server. It does not wait for a new help request because it is already committed to help some other agent at that particular step. Note that, as the last agent has picked an action (the one that requested help), all agents are free to send their actions.

However, an agent could take a long time to come up to a conclusion; whether help is required or not. In this sense, we draw a line on how much time agents should wait for that request. The agents wait for one second before sending its action to the server. After that deadline, no agent will help another at that particular step, they must wait for the next one. With this approach we can minimise useless actions being performed in the environment in case the agent's commitment to goals has changed.

4.2   Battery Management

Each movement (goto) action that a vehicle performs costs a certain amount of battery, as defined by the match parameters. An agent has two options for recharging its battery: using the recharge action or going to one of the charging station facilities in the map and executing the charge action. The former can be used anywhere in the map to try to recharge the vehicle's battery by using its solar panels, but it is not reliable since it has a chance of failure, and even if it succeeds, only recharges a small amount of battery. The latter requires the vehicle to be in a charging station facility, but it is much more reliable and will recharge the battery rapidly (each charging station has its own recharge rate that represents the amount of battery restored in one step).

Our agents take a preemptive approach to decide when to visit charging stations to recharge their battery. Whenever an agent has a goal to move to a different position (either a facility or a specific coordinate), it checks if it has enough battery to arrive in its destination and go to the charging station that is closest to that goal. If that is not possible, then the agent calculates a path between its current position and its goal that would allow this condition to be true, visiting as many charging stations as necessary. A more detailed algorithm is presented in our team description of the MAPC 2016 [11].

In the MAPC 2017 [10], our agents sent the recharge action whenever they were idle, but in the current edition (MAPC 2018) our agents would rarely find themselves idle. This, along with the changes to the recharge action (increased

---

[3] We assume agents cannot simply override their sent actions because once the server has received all expected actions it advances to the next step.

chance of failure and lower amount of battery recovered), resulted in more visits to charging stations. The `recharge` action was only used when our agents were idle or if they had zero battery.

Pruning the List of Charging Stations. Agents make constant use of the list of charging stations that are available in the map. For example, they use it to decide which charging stations to visit (this happens every time an agent decides to move to some coordinates), or to estimate their bid for a task in a contract net (this also happens very frequently). This results in multiple calls to the internal action used to obtain which charging station is close to certain coordinates (e.g., the agent's current position, the position of the agent's destination, etc.), and each call would need to calculate, from the list of all possible charging stations, the route length from those coordinates to each charging station. Thus, in maps that have a large number of charging stations (i.e., more than 30), calculating which one is closest proved to be computationally expensive when dealing with all of the 34 agents available in MAPC 2018.

To solve this problem, in the start of a simulation round we removed all charging stations that were close to each other. We had to determine what "close" meant, and it is important to note that this was a quick fix made during the contest to ensure that our team could work in large maps, such as the one in the third round of the contest (the São Paulo map had more than 50 charging stations). In our solution, close refers to at least ten steps (this number was obtained from testing in the contest maps with 50+ charging stations), considering the default movement speed of a truck vehicle. For example, in a map with 50 charging stations, we loop through each charging station (C_i), calculate which charging station is closest (C_i') to C_i, calculate the route length from C_i to C_i', and remove C_i' if the route length is at least 10 steps away from C_i. In contrast, previous editions had a much lower number of agents and facilities (28 agents and approximately 10 charging stations in the third round of MAPC 2017).

4.3 Centre Facilities

Our assemble and delivery strategy mainly depends on the place we chose to store our items. We did not have enough time to develop an algorithm that takes into account many storage to decide where is the best location to retrieve and store items. Therefore, we decided to use a centralised storage to store all items (i.e., base and compound items). However, just choosing the closest storage to the centre of the map was not sufficient because our agents may spend many steps in locomotion from one place to another; in this sense, a centre workshop should be chosen as well.

We choose those facilities based on the route from the map central coordinates to the storage plus workshop distance. The lowest route indicates which storage and workshop should be chosen as central facilities. Once those were chosen, our agents always use them to complete their tasks.

4.4 Gathering

In contrast to most other types of facilities which have their position known at the start of the simulation, the location of resource nodes is not initially known. An agent receives the location of a resource node if there are any nodes inside its vision radius. When a new resource node is discovered it is added to the team artefact so that all agents in the team have access to its parameters (the coordinates and the item's name).

Because a team has 34 agents, it is usually the case that when the simulation of a round starts there are at least some resource nodes known from the initial position of the agents. However, this is not always true, as in our tests we found some configurations with no initial resource nodes. If there are no initial resource nodes available, the gatherers move to a random known facility to aid in the exploration, and then check if any resource nodes have been discovered.

If there are resource nodes available, then an agent selects the most requested base item in the desired base-item list and goes to the closest resource node that has that base item (there can be multiple resource nodes with the same item). The most requested base item is defined as the base item that is used the most in the assembly of the items required by jobs. After the agent finishes gathering the item, it then unloads it on the agreed centre storage.

An agent can choose a particular resource to gather in two different situations: after the agent has stored the resource it gathered and the desired base-item list changed, or when a new resource node is detected. In both cases the resource node selection strategy remains the same.

4.5 Upgrades

All of our agents have the ability to upgrade. However, the decision to upgrade depends on the strategy adopted by the team as a whole, since they share the same massium quantity. The upgrades available to the agents are: speed, load, skill, vision, and battery. To decide whether an agent should perform an upgrade, it first checks if it has not reached the maximum skill value of its MAPC role (each MAPC role has its own maximum value for each skill) and if the team has enough massium. If an upgrade is needed, the agent goes to the nearest shop and performs the upgrade action stating which upgrade it desires.

4.6 Building Wells

The main purpose of the game is to build wells, but this is not always possible due to lack of massium. When building a well is not possible, the agents that have this duty walk around the map. The reason for this strategy is twofold: (i) it helps to discover adversarial wells; (ii) it spreads the agents throughout the map, and as a consequence our wells are geographically well spread (i.e., they are built on very different positions of the map).

When the agents perceive that they have enough massium to build a well, they move forward to the closest map boundary. We always build wells on the edges of the map because it demands more steps for the opponent team's agents to get to that location. The first agent to reach a boundary of the map will be able to build the well. This agent will choose a well type according to the available `massium` and our ranking list of well types. This list is designed taking into account the cost and the efficiency of each type of well. Without `massium`, the agents go back to walking around the map.

Sometimes, it can happen that there exists already a building on the position that an agent wants to build a well. When this happens, the agent plans a route to the farthest facility and sends only one `goto` action towards it. If the next position also has a building in it, the agent repeats the procedure until it finds a free location to build a well.

4.7   Attacking

When a new adversarial well is discovered, by any agent, it is added to the team artefact. In this sense, all agents will know exactly the location of that well. Agents are not attackers by design, they become attackers when some situation is perceived in the environment (e.g., an adversarial well is discovered). Some roles allow their agents to become attackers as long as they are not performing an important task (e.g., building a well).

Agents choose the closest well to go to destroy among the ones listed in the team artefact. However, they can reconsider an attack in the light of new wells being discovered, as long as they are still in route (i.e., have the desire to go to some well). They always choose the closest one. Once a well is destroyed, this well is removed from the team artefact and, if there is no other well to attack, the agents return to their previous role and activities.

To attack a well when few agents are allowed to attack (for more details see Sect. 5.3) upgrades play an important role. An upgrade demands `massium`, but it helps to improve attack behaviour. We only need this strategy when the number of attacker are constrained to few agents, so our attack power is limited.

4.8   Items Management

We delegate to the *initiator* the responsibility to evaluate whether it is necessary to gather base items or to assemble compound items. Now, we describe all aspects that we have used to reason about items.

Stock Management. We use a single centralised storage facility to store the items collected/assembled during the simulation. Base items can be collected in the environment whereas compound items need to be assembled from other items. Both item types (base and compound) are stored at the same facility and logically maintained in two priority lists in the `TeamArtifact`. We update items per job; every time a new job is announced the desired stock quantity is updated according to the maximum amount of item required by all jobs seen so far. That way, we try to keep in stock a greater quantity of the items that are more likely to be required in future jobs.

Perhaps this is better explained with an example. Consider a simulation in which we have three types of compounded items, say type 1CI, 2CI, and 3CI. The first job announced requires two 1CI; at this moment we register in the quantity list of compounded items (QLCI) the tuple (2, 0, 0). The next job requires one 1CI, one 2CI, then the QLCI is updated to (2, 1, 0). A job that requires five 3CI is announced, so the QLCI is updated to (2, 1, 5). In this sense, we are prepared to deliver the worst case of jobs we have seen so far.

Once we have evaluated the desired quantities, each agent selects a base item to gather based on a probability. The probability depends on its stored quantity and the desired stock quantity for this item. So, base items with lower stock quantity compared to its desired stock quantity will have a higher chance to be gathered (the same principle is used to define which compounded item should be assembled).

Assembling Allocation. As we use a centralised storage, allocation process is easier to evaluate. Indeed, our main goal is to transport a number of items from one place to another. For this purpose we use the CNP [18]. Every time a new base item is stored or a compounded item is removed from stock, the initiator evaluates if the stock amount of required items is enough; if it is not, the initiator reasons about what compounded items are needed at the moment and if the base items are available. This is done by comparing the real stock quantities of compounded items with the desired amount. If a particular compound item is far from its desired quantity, it receives higher priority in assembling.

The agents that are able to participate in this process must play the role of `gatherer` or `explorer_drone`; each of them will provide a bid to the initiator indicating how suitable they are for the tasks. The `explorer_drone` is necessary because most compound items require `drones` to be assembled; and the `gatherer` role usually has the remaining types of agents. Each bid contains the agent available load, type, and route length (in steps) to the centre storage, to the centre workshop, and back to the centre storage. With that information, the initiator can infer how many compound items can be assembled and how much volume can be transported. After that, for each compound item (sorted in a priority list), the initiator checks if the available agents can assemble it. If so, it decomposes the compound item in tasks (for the base items quantities) and sorts the agents according to their route lengths to the facilities. After that, it selects a subset of agents that are capable of transporting the total volume of base items and allocate to them the tasks to assemble the compound item. If the item cannot be assembled, it takes the next item in the priority list. In this process, the initiator also indicates which agent is responsible for sending the `assemble` action. The final duty of the initiator in this process is to update the stock amount, so that it will not use allocated items for future allocation processes.

Note that, if the allocation process fails for any reason, we pick the next item in the priority list and repeat the process. If no item could be assembled at the moment (e.g., base items are missing), we only start the process again when a new base item is stored, meaning our storage state has changed.

Assembling Compound Items. All agents that have won at least one task contract are notified and start to work on accomplishing them. To do so, they must commit to missions in the assembling scheme (see Sect. 2.3 and Fig. 1). Each agent chosen by the initiator to perform the action `assemble` for a particular compound item will create a $\mathcal{M}$OISE group to assemble that item and will adopt the `assembler` role in this temporary group. It also creates a scheme for coordinating the assembly process. The agents that will help to assemble the compound item adopt the `assistant` role. The *assembler* must be committed to the missions to retrieve items and assemble item. The *assistant* role will be committed to the mission to retrieve items and assist the assembler. It is important to note that finishing the mission to retrieve items is the synchronisation point among the agents because all of them will be at the workshop and can start sending the respective actions to assemble the compound item. After assembling the item, the assembler agent delivers it to the destination storage. The remaining agents go back to their previous roles and activities.

Full Storage. During a match, a storage could get full of items due to (i) the number of required items in our stock; (ii) the adversary team's strategy. This situation could brake our team because we use a central storage (chosen at the beginning of the simulation), and once this storage is full the agents will not be able to assemble more items and even deliver jobs (e.g., new jobs may require compound items that are out of stock). To be ready for this cumbersome situation, we prepared a contingency strategy in which the initiator chooses the second nearest storage to the centre of the map, and the agents start to use only that storage. All items stored in the previous storage are ignored by our agents, and a new stock is built.

4.9   Delivering Jobs

Jobs are essential to earn money in order to build wells, although completing them is a difficult challenge. To deliver a job we need to gather *base items* to assemble *compound items* that are job requirements. In this sense, we only accept jobs if we have already fulfilled their requirements (i.e, the required items are already stored in the centre storage). We delegate to the *initiator* the responsibility to evaluate and allocate all types of job (we only consider priced jobs and missions).

Job Allocation. The allocation of jobs is simpler than the assembling allocation. As we also have to transport items from one storage to another, the initiator only opens one CNP for each job delivery. Agents that play the roles *gatherer* or *explorer* will be notified about the CNP. Their bids are evaluated considering their route to the centre storage (to retrieve required items) and to the destination storage (to deliver items). Moreover, they also should take into account the detour to charging stations and the time to fully charge their batteries, if necessary. An accepted job will be decomposed into several tasks according to the number of items required by it. After receiving the bids, the initiator starts allocating tasks to the agents. First, it orders the bid list according to the route length to the facilities. Then it evaluates how many steps are needed, in worst case, to transport the items from one storage to another. Based on the total load of the required items, it starts summing up the agent's free load on the ordered list until the free load be greater than the total load of items required for that job. The agent with largest route length in this set poses the step constraint. Note that, we can have more than one slowest agent (i.e., largest route length). As we want to use as few agents as possible, the initiator orders the bid list of the selected agents according to their free load choosing the agents of larger load to accomplish the job.

The difference between *priced jobs* and *missions* is as follows. In the former, every time a new priced job is announced, the initiator checks if the required items are available and starts the allocation process. For the missions, if the mission is infeasible, the initiator keeps the mission in mind and tries to allocate it every time a new compound item is added to the centre stock. If the mission deadline is too short (e.g., 30 steps to conclude) the initiator does not try to allocate it anymore. Although we did have strategies for `auction jobs`, we were not able to fully implement them as part of the team due to lack of time.

Now that we have detailed our task allocation process, we introduce a running example of how Jason meta-events (Sect. 2.1) could be applied to solve the problem of selecting which type of allocation process to do first when various are enabled. Assume that during a step we have a mission opened and not allocated yet, a regular job is announced, and an agent stored a base item in the storage in the previous step. All tasks are allocated to the agents by the *initiator*. This agent is responsible for starting the allocation processes in three distinct moments, taking into account the following priority order: (i) when there are enough items in stock to complete a mission; (ii) when there are enough items in stock to deliver a priced job (regular job); (iii) when there are enough base items in stock to assemble a compound item. Since all conditions are satisfied in our hypothetical step above, three intentions are created in our initiator agent, which must allocate one process at a time in order not to allocate the same agent to conflicting jobs (e.g., an agent receives tasks for delivering a regular job and assembling a compound item at the same time).

We explain how the initiator selects an allocation process to execute based on Listing 1.1. Three intentions are generated and thus three meta-events are created announcing state `started` ($\land$ symbol in line 1); note that all meta-events are processed before checking the context of any other plan. If there is no intention trying to execute the allocation process or if the intention has the

```
1   ^!pick_task(G)[priority(MyP),state(started)]
2    : not task_priority(_) | (task_priority(P) & MyP < P)
3   <- -+task_priority(MyP).
4   +!pick_task(G)[priority(MyP)]
5    : not requesting_help & (not task_priority(_) |
6                              (task_priority(P) & MyP <= P))
7   <- +requesting_help;
8      !G;
9      -task_priority(_);
10      -requesting_help.
11  +!pick_task(G)[priority(P)]
12  <- .wait({-requesting_help});
13      !pick_task(G)[priority(P)].
```

Listing 1.1. Example of the use of Jason meta-events.

highest priority (lower value in line 2), then we update the belief (using the $-+$ operator) with the new highest priority (line 3). The intention with the highest priority adds a belief indicating the beginning of the allocation process and executes the intended goal. Once the goal has finished (by success or failure), it removes the beliefs indicating the highest priority and allocation execution (lines 7–10). If the intention does not have the highest priority, then it gets to state suspended until belief requesting_help is removed. After that, it is allowed to enter state started and starts over the procedure (back to line 1). This procedure ensures that only one task allocation process will be executed at time.

Delivery Failures. The agents that have tasks assigned to them change their roles to delivery_agent and go to the centre storage to retrieve the items they are responsible for. After that, they go straight to the destination storage to deliver the items. Once this is done, delivery agents are free to return to their previous role and regular activities. However, in some situations (e.g., the job deadline has passed, or the other team has delivered the job first) our job delivery fails. For those situations we have two possibilities: (i) the agent has made a partial delivery; and (ii) the agent is on its way to the storage. For (i), the agent does not try to get the delivered items back, it leaves them in the storage. For (ii), the agent returns to the centre storage and stores all items it is carrying. After one of the two cases, the agent is free to change back roles.

4.10   Changing the Round

A match in the MAPC is formed by three rounds, each round with its own map and parameters. The round transition is seamless from the server perspective, meaning that there is no downtime between rounds, and as soon as one round ends the next one begins. Although it is possible to disconnect the team at the end of a round and then reconnect again at the start of a new round, we wanted our agents to be able to autonomously adapt to a round change.

Our environment artefact automatically updates all environment perceptions. However, there are many beliefs and intentions that would otherwise carry over to a new round. Our agents do not want to simply erase everything, since there are artefacts, organisation, and parameter belief's that they need regardless of which round it is. Thus, at the end of each round, an agent will abolish[4] all beliefs, except the ones from the `default` namespace, which is where the beliefs that we want to keep cross-rounds are kept.

At the end of the round, agents drop all their current desires, which in turn removes all the current intentions. On a new round, agents set the map parameters according to the percepts sent by the server at the start of that round.

5   Match Analysis

In this section we analyse our performance against teams that had the highest score in the contest: Jason-DTU (third place), Dumping to Gather (fourth place), and TUBDAI (second place). Our team tied for second place with TUBDAI. Table 1 shows the overall score in each map for these matches. The number on the right-hand side is our score. For example, consider the match against Jason-DTU in Copenhagen. The score for Jason-DTU was 3644 and we got 6800. Each match had three rounds and each round had a different map (Copenhagen, Berlin, and São Paulo)[5].

Table 1. Overall scores by map; our scores are on the right-hand side; bold font indicates the winner of the round.

Rival Team	Copenhagen	Berlin	São Paulo
Jason-DTU	3644 : **6800**	**9142** : 7079	770 : **41324**
Dumping to Gather	2303 : **4581**	9163 : **62413**	4367 : **29543**
TUBDAI	515 : **2337**	1808 : **5098**	600 : **2598**

In Fig. 3, we show the score earned by all teams for each map averaged across all matches in the contest. TUBDAI did a little better than our team in the first map (the smallest map). Our team has the best average by far in Berlin and São Paulo, the largest and most difficult maps in MAPC 2018.

---

[4] This is an agent internal action provided by Jason to remove all beliefs that match the action's argument.

[5] The reader can see all the matches replays at https://multiagentcontest.org/2018/.

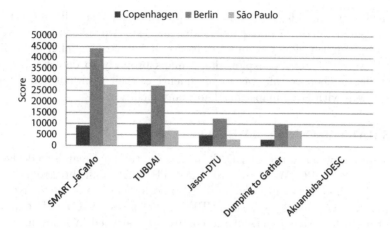

Fig. 3. Score earned in each map round averaged across all matches.

5.1 SMART_JaCaMo x Jason-DTU

Our first match was against the Jason-DTU team. We lost the second round (map of Berlin) to them; this was also the only round we lost in the 2018 contest. In the first round, we won with a difference in score of 3156 points. Jason-DTU used similar strategies to ours. They attacked our wells, completed jobs, and built wells on map boundaries. The most different aspect between the two teams related to the exploration. Their explorers (drones) conducted a triangle format search on each map boundary instead of following a straight line from one corner to another.

We were winning the second round until step 879. We lost this round because our `builders` were prioritising dismantling wells instead of building new ones. For instance, at step 345 we had enough `massium` to build new wells, but we did not do it. We fixed this bug and our builders started to prioritise the construction of wells, and only attacked wells when there was not enough `massium` to build new wells.

We had another bug in the third round, in the map of São Paulo. This was a very large map with many charging stations in it. Our agents were very slow due to the evaluation of routes. To evaluate a route we take into account the available charging stations in the map. We fixed this by limiting the number of charging stations we considered in the evaluation (for further details see Sect. 4.2).

5.2 SMART_JaCaMo x Dumping to Gather

We won all three rounds against Dumping to Gather. The first round was relatively close compared to the last two. In the first round the score difference was much lower due to the small map size and lower number of facilities. This map resulted in wells that could easily be discovered and attacked without impacting the other activities of the agents, such as building and completing jobs.

In the last two rounds, our team ended up with 64 and 124 wells (respectively) when compared to their 7 and 2 wells. This suggests two things: they were not able to win as much money to build wells due to the large number of facilities, and they were not able to explore large maps properly to detect and attack enemy wells. We believe this was a consequence of their team not being able to cope very well with large maps that had many facilities.

5.3   SMART_JaCaMo x TUBDAI

Our last match was against TUBDAI, and it was the final match to decide the winner of 2018 MAPC. We needed to defeat TUBDAI in all three rounds to be declared the winner; if we lost one round then both teams would tie for 1st place.

It was a tough match because TUBDAI used a completely different "approach" than other participants in the contest. It consisted in building wells in places that only drones would be able to access. The *GraphHopper API* was used by the MAPC server to calculate routes and, due to its limitations, a valid route for ground vehicles (all except drones) meant that there must be a route, not necessarily a street route since *all agents* can indeed move over field and water, between the current position and the goal position of the vehicle. The point is, some routes were invalid only for ground vehicles at a few particular locations in all maps. This was an *undocumented feature* of the contest and we believe it was poor sportsmanship of that team to try and exploit teams that were not aware of this flaw or, as in our case, knew about it but made the ethical decision to play correctly in accordance with the purpose of the competition rather than using such a trick as an easy way to win the competition without having to build intelligent agents that are able to solve the hard problem that was effectively posed to contestants.

Note, for example, that if all teams decided to take advantage of such undocumented feature or flaw (which of course most contestants realised), only drones would be used to build and attack wells, while other types of agents would be limited to contributing to jobs. This would go against, for example, exploiting the heterogeneity of the roles in the proposed scenario, and more generally would mean the whole problem created by the organisers of the competition would be seriously compromised, in the sense that the produced solutions would have little use for solving similar problems in real applications.

By observing TUBDAI strategy in their previous matches, we took advantage of our role-based implementation approach and adapted our strategy to counter attack it. In previous matches, our drones were prioritised for exploration and item delivery for jobs; since each team only has four drones, it is a scarce resource. Our adaptation for this match was to switch priorities so that no matter what the drones were doing, they would prioritise exploration and attacking wells instead. They also upgrade the `skill` attribute to be able to increase their attack power. The other agents remained the same, except that they only decided to attack a well if there was a valid route to it.

However, even prioritising drones to attack wells we still had disadvantages in facing TUBDAI. We built our wells in the normal map coordinates, therefore accessible to any vehicle. Consequently, any TUBDAI agent could attack them (drones, motorcycle, cars, and trucks). Conversely, all of ours agents, except drones, were not able to attack TUBDAI wells.

We had a stable implementation and only had to reconnect once in the final match, due to latency problems. The movement of our builders throughout the map allowed us to build our wells spread out; this cost TUBDAI agents many steps for attacking our wells. Our team was *dynamic* and the positions where we built wells was *unpredictable*. We believe this was a key feature in our victory in all three rounds.

In the end, despite having the highest score after all matches, a decision was made that our team should be tied in second place alongside TUBDAI. After the contest, TUBDAI formally requested to the MAPC organisers to reevaluate the results of our match. They stated we should not have configured our drones to prioritise attacking wells, because "drastic code changes" were not allowed in between matches during the contest. One of the best features of our code this year was to be modular and adaptable. Through the dynamic use of a Moise organisations we were able to change our agents' behaviour by swapping roles and priorities. Because of the quality of our code, the changes to win this match required mostly reconfiguring the team roles, it required virtually no actual programming, so we did not consider this as breaking rule that major changes in code were not allowed during the competition (fixing normal bugs, which is allowed, almost invariable requires a lot more programming than this, and it should be noted that, historically, significant reprogramming of team strategies has been conducted in practice by many teams in the MAPC, which has always been taken in good sport by all participants, an in line with the competition purpose). We claim that this ease way to reconfigure the roles of agents in the team is an important feature to have in many MAS applications and that teams should not be restricted from solving these challenges; instead, strategies that capitalise on map-specific details or undocumented problems that might be overlooked by some teams should be the ones to be discouraged.

6   Team Overview: Short Answers

6.1   Participants and Their Background

What was your motivation to participate in the contest?
Our main motivation was to improve our knowledge about agent technologies, and put them into practice in a complex multi-agent scenario. We also wanted to compare how effective a JaCaMo implementation could be against other agent development platforms and discover improvements that could be made.

What is the history of your group?
Most of our members are from the SMART (Semantic, Multi-Agent, and Robotic Technologies) research group at PUCRS. Our main research is in the area of multi-agent systems, but also on other aspects of Artificial Intelligence such as argumentation, knowledge representation using formal ontologies, multi-agent planning. This is our third participation in the MAPC.

What is your field of research? Which work therein is related?
All of our members have a background in Computer Science, and more specifically Artificial Intelligence. Research topics include, but are not limited to: Mulit-Agent Oriented Programming, Automated Planning, Multi-Agent Planning, Coalition Formation, Task Allocation, Argumentation, and Ontologies. The deadline to send an action in each step severely limits the applicability of most of the approaches developed by our research group, for example decentralised planning [9] and task allocation [3] techniques[6], although basic concepts from these topics guided many of our ideas.

6.2 Development

How much time did you invest in the contest for (for programming, organization your group, other)?
Approximately 200 h. It includes time spent in meetings, programming, testing, and so on. We used our code developed for the 2017 MAPC as a basis, which in turn was based on our code from 2016 (all were in the same scenario). These 200 h were used mostly for improving significantly upon our previous code, by adding many features required for the new edition of the scenario.

How many lines of code did you produce for your final agent team?
Our final agent team had 6109 lines of code in total, which is approximately double of what we had in the previous MAPC (2017). From this total, we had 3176 lines of agent code, 1234 lines in configuration files, and 1699 lines of Java code. Measurements were taken using Linux wc command plus sed for removing blank lines. It should be noted that comments and extra lines that we used to improve code readability were not removed in the numbers reported above.

How many people were involved and to which degree?
Our team consisted of 8 participants: two MSc students, three PhD students, one postdoctoral researcher, and two collaborators.

When did you start working on your agents?
We started working on this project on the 11th of April, 2018.

6.3 System Details

How do your agents work together? (coordination, information sharing, ...)
Coordination for job allocation is based on contract net protocol. An initiator is responsible for decomposing items, evaluating jobs, announcing tasks, and allocating tasks to winners. Coordination for task execution is done through the specification of Moise schemes (i.e., sets of structured social/global goals).

---

[6] Usually, there is state space explosion in such problems, which means finding the best solution (or at least a bound from the best solution) is often not feasible online and with short response time as required for the MAPC.

We also use an artefact that all agents can access to share important information. For example, the agent sends the information that it wants to share with the team to the TeamArtifact, which is focused by all agents in the team.

What are critical components of your team?

The main components of our team are: each agent's environment artefact, the contract net protocol artefacts, the team artefact, and the social schemes from the $\mathcal{M}$OISE organisation. The main strategies used by our team are: exploring the map, task allocation, coordinating agents when retrieving the same type of item or when current intentions are changed, coordination of task execution, battery recharge, and attacking wells.

Can your agents change their behavior during runtime? If so, what triggers the changes?

In our team we use Jason internal actions to drop an agent's desires and intentions. When a new intention appears (e.g., due to environment changes) for any given step, past intentions that aimed to send an action to the contest server are dropped in favour of the most recent intention.

Did you have to make changes to the team (e.g. fix critical bugs) during the contest?

During the contest we only did minor bug fixes and optimisation of a few execution parameters. We also had a particular issue related to TUBDAI match, as detailed in Sect. 5.3.

How do you organize your agents? Do you use e.g. hierarchies? Is your organization implicit or explicit?

There are two organisation hierarchies in our team. Agents receive a base role when the simulation starts; it is defined a priori. They may change roles depending on the state of the environment (see Sect. 4). However, agents may also organise themselves in connection to particular jobs. Agents that are allocated to the task of assembling items form another group having secondary roles to play. During task allocation, one of the drone agents plays the role of initiator, but it is also allowed to place bids.

Is most of your agents' behavior emergent on an individual or team level?

The behaviour is highly adaptive to the state of the environment, but not "emergent". Most of the developed behaviour was created at the individual level, but we do have a few team aspects for coordination and control purposes, such as which agents are awarded with more than one task, and which ones are able to retrieve items from the storage. We also have a explicit team level behaviour defined by $\mathcal{M}$OISE schemes.

If your agents perform some planning, how many steps do they plan ahead?

We developed code that can plan ahead the full route, including any stops to recharge battery. This was not the case in our participation of previous MAPCs, where our agents ignored charging stops during their initial plan to bid for tasks. Thus, each agent plans the whole execution before bidding to do a task.

If you have a perceive-think-act cycle, how is it synchronized with the server?

Synchronisation with the server is done through each agent's artefact, on a step-by-step basis. These artefacts receive perceptions from the server, filter the ones related to their agent, discard any information that the agent has no use for, and then send them to their respective agent. The agent reasons about the information received, chooses an appropriate action and sends it to their artefact, which finally sends it to the server.

How did you go about debugging your system?

Throughout the development phase, we used GitHub to collaborate and track our progress. We used it for tracking bugs, task assignment, version control, and especially for developing multiple strategies in different branches, and then testing them separately and adding the best ones to the master branch.

Which operating system did you use, and is your team portable to other operating systems?

We used Ubuntu 16.04 to run our code. Our agents are portable to any other operating system as long as it has Java installed. It is one of the benefits of using the JaCaMo platform.

What hardware did you use to run your agent team? (RAM, CPU, disk space, multiple computers, any other notable requirements)

We used an Apple MacPro5, 2 Hexa Core Intel Xeon 2.40 GHz, 32 Gb RAM (DDR3 1333MHz), 3 TB HDD, NVidia Titan Xp.

6.4 Scenario and Strategy

What is the main strategy of your agent team?

We have two main strategies. The first is to use contract net protocol for task allocation, so that the agents themselves can decide who is best for the tasks that a particular job requires. The second is to use an organisation structure to coordinate item assembly, resource gathering, building wells, exploring the map, and attacking wells.

How do your agents decide which jobs to complete?

The contract net initiator first checks if the required compound items are in stock. If so, it starts a CNP to choose agents to deliver the job at the right storage.

Do you have different strategies for the different roles?

The types of vehicle have an impact in each agent's bid during task allocation for jobs. Vehicles that move faster tend to have a smaller route length estimate, making their bids more favourable, as long as they can carry all items needed for the task. Our drones prioritise map exploration and attacking wells, although this can be easily reconfigured.

Do your agents form ad-hoc teams to complete a task?

The team responsible for assembling a compound item is formed of all CNP winners related to that item. These agents should, in principle, be the best ones available for the task.

How do your agents decide when and where to build wells?

Our agents always build wells at the beginning of each round, if there is enough money. There is also two occasions that they could decide to build a well: (i) after completing jobs; and (ii) after destroying opponent's wells. Our wells are always built on the boundaries of the map.

If your agents accumulated a lot of currency, why did they not spend it immediately?

It could be that they are far from the boundaries of the map; or that they are saving currency for more expensive wells; or that they are busy with other tasks with higher priority (such as attacking wells).

6.5   And the Moral of It Is ...

What did you learn from participating in the contest?

We have improved our knowledge of agent technologies, in particular JaCaMo programming, and how agent techniques can be applied in such a complex scenario.

What are the strong and weak points of your team?

We believe our strongest point is the use of a role-based implementation. We can change significantly our team's strategy by changing only a few lines of code. Our weakest point is the use of a centralised storage for stocking items.

How viable were your chosen programming language, methodology, tools, and algorithms?

We did not have any major problems programming our agent team in JaCaMo. The use of Github for source code management, access control, and collaboration features, such as bug tracking and wikis, made it a lot easier to manage our team more efficiently.

Did you encounter new problems during the contest?

There are a lot of random elements in this scenario, making it harder to properly test all of our team's code. We had a few minor bugs, but the most troublesome was dealing with large maps with lots of facilities, with each step of the simulation making our system slower. To solve this, especially in the São Paulo map, we had to prune our list of charging stations in order to run our agents properly.

Did playing against other agent teams bring about new insights on your own agents?

During the matches with TUBDAI, we observed that their wells were located in positions accessible only by drones, making it impossible for other agents to attack. This situation confirmed how easy it was to adapt our team's strategies by just switching the roles of our agents.

What would you improve if you wanted to participate in the same contest a week from now (or next year)?

We would finish implementing missing features. For instance, we did not finish the implementation of bidding for auctions. Also, we would like to decentralise the storage we use for stocking items, but this would require a new strategy to store and assemble items.

Which aspect of your team cost you the most time?

Developing our assemble strategy, our approach to task allocation (CNP), dealing with concurrent intentions within the agent's mental state, and making sure that our code worked in as many different situations as possible.

Why did your team perform as it did? Why did the other teams perform better/worse than you did?

Our role-based approach was safe and straightforward. We defined each agent's role according to the scenario's requirement, but also reacting to the environment.

6.6 The Future of the MAPC

What can be improved regarding the contest for next year?

We believe the qualification phase is outdated. Instead of just testing the connection of a team to the contest's server, it should also make sure that the team can accomplish a task; the task here depends on the scenario, for example, it could be completing a job and building a well in the MAPC 2018 scenario (starting with zero currency).

What kind of scenario would you like to play next? What kind of features should the new scenario have?

We think it would be interesting if the next scenario was aligned with hard problems addressing current industrial challenges (e.g., smart cities, industry 4.0, etc.). A feature that would bring more diversity and new challenges would be to have more interactions between agents of different teams. For example, sabotaging enemy agents (as in the Mars scenario of past years), trading items with the other team, or even some kind of cooperative action that could benefit both teams. We also think open MAS is a very interesting and difficult topic to be addressed as well.

Should the teams be allowed to make changes to their agents during the contest (even based on opponent agent behavior observed in earlier matches)? If yes, should only some changes be legal and which ones (e.g. bugfixes), and how to decide a change's classification? If no, should we ensure that no changes are made and how?

Teams should be allowed to make any changes they want to their code during the matches, as indeed it has happened in practice since the beginning of the MAPC. Note that if the point of the competition was to have the code fully complete before the start, as in some other AI competitions, there would be benchmarks for testing and organisers would collect the code before the start and run it themselves then just report the winner. Instead, this competition has always favoured allowing teams to use the time of the competition itself to improve their own code. This is the whole "fun" of the MAPC.

Real-world environments are extremely dynamic and MAS solutions should be able to autonomously adapt its behaviour, as well as to allow human operators to make the required changes as fast as possible. For instance, for a self-driving car, human operators will certainly want to change agent code when the car is being serviced. In some applications indeed human intervention is not possible at all time. That is why we are programming autonomous agents, but in any case it should certainly be allowed whenever needed. Restricting this means in practice to constrain creative solutions that promote modularity and adaptability, both important features in MAS.

Do you have ideas to reduce the impact of unforeseen strategies (e.g., playing a second leg after some time)?

The organisation should not make any attempt to address this issue. The teams themselves should be able to adapt and counter attack potentially questionable strategies. Most importantly, for this very reason, the organisers must not schedule all matches of only one of the teams for the very last day of the competition. This implies all teams know all other team strategies except the favoured team that happened to be scheduled to play only the final matches.

7 Conclusion

The organisers have managed to make the *Agents in the City* scenario the most challenging problem yet. Our team managed to solve almost every part of this brilliant competition problem. Following the strategy of last year's winning team, the BusyBeaver, our team only accepts new jobs when all required items for that job are available in stock. At first, our team cannot deliver jobs, but after some steps, we can possibly deliver jobs faster than the adversarial teams.

Furthermore, our team strategy was based mainly on organisational roles from MOISE. Using those roles we can enable new abilities in our agents by simply allowing them to take a new role; this is essentially a change in one line of code. In future work, we intend to make this role changing more dynamic at run-time. MOISE was also used for the coordination of the agents during complex jobs. We also improved the Jason programming of our agents. This year, we focused on manipulating agent's desires and intentions in order to reach its changing goals. We also mention our separation of simple behaviour from higher-level strategies and the use of Jason modules as an important feature to keep our code easy to be developed. The 2018 MAPC was a very interesting contest and we hope the next one will be even more challenging.

References

1. Ahlbrecht, T., Dix, J., Fiekas, N.: Multi-agent programming contest 2016. Int. J. Agent-Oriented Softw. Eng. **6**(1), 55–85 (2018)
2. Ahlbrecht, T., Dix, J., Fiekas, N.: Multi-agent programming contest 2017. Ann. Math. Artif. Intell. **84**(1–2), 1–16 (2018)
3. Baségio, T.L., Bordini, R.H.: Allocating structured tasks in heterogeneous agent teams. Comput. Intell. **35**(1), 124–155 (2019)
4. Behrens, T.M., Hindriks, K.V., Dix, J.: Towards an environment interface standard for agent platforms. Ann. Math. Artif. Intell. **61**(4), 261–295 (2011)
5. Boissier, O., Bordini, R.H., Hübner, J.F., Ricci, A., Santi, A.: Multi-agent oriented programming with JaCaMo. Sci. Comput. Prog. **78**(6), 747–761 (2013)

6. Bordini, R.H., Hübner, J.F., Wooldridge, M.: Programming Multi-Agent Systems in AgentSpeak using Jason. Wiley, Hoboken (2007)
7. Bratman, M.E., Israel, D.J., Pollack, M.E.: Plans and resource-bounded practical reasoning. Comput. Intell. **4**(3), 349–355 (1988)
8. Braubach, L., Pokahr, A., Moldt, D., Lamersdorf, W.: Goal representation for BDI agent systems. In: Bordini, R.H., Dastani, M., Dix, J., El Fallah Seghrouchni, A. (eds.) ProMAS 2004. LNCS (LNAI), vol. 3346, pp. 44–65. Springer, Heidelberg (2005). https://doi.org/10.1007/978-3-540-32260-3_3
9. Cardoso, R.C., Bordini, R.H.: Decentralised planning for multi-agent programming platforms. In: Proceedings of the International Conference on Autonomous Agents and MultiAgent Systems, pp. 799–818, Richland (2019)
10. Cardoso, R.C., Krausburg, T., Baségio, T., Engelmann, D.C., Hübner, J.F., Bordini, R.H.: SMART-JaCaMo: an organization-based team for the multi-agent programming contest. Ann. Math. Artif. Intell. **84**(1), 75–93 (2018)
11. Cardoso, R.C., Pereira, R.F., Krzisch, G., Magnaguagno, M.C., Baségio, T., Meneguzzi, F.: Team PUCRS: a decentralised multi-agent solution for the agents in the city scenario. Int. J. Agent-Oriented Softw. Eng. **6**(1), 3–34 (2018)
12. Rocha Costa, A.C.: Two concepts of module, for agent societies and inter-societal agent systems. In: El Fallah-Seghrouchni, A., Ricci, A., Son, T.C. (eds.) EMAS 2017. LNCS (LNAI), vol. 10738, pp. 56–72. Springer, Cham (2018). https://doi.org/10.1007/978-3-319-91899-0_4
13. Hübner, J.F., Sichman, J.S., Boissier, O.: Developing organised multiagent systems using the moise+ model: programming issues at the system and agent levels. Int. J. Agent-Oriented Softw. Eng. **1**(3/4), 370–395 (2007)
14. Omicini, A., Ricci, A., Viroli, M.: Artifacts in the A&A meta-model for multi-agent systems. Auton. Agents Multi-Agent Syst. **17**(3), 432–456 (2008)
15. Rao A.S.: AgentSpeak(L): BDI agents speak out in a logical computable language. In: Van de Velde, W., Perram, J.W. (eds.) Agents Breaking Away. MAAMAW 1996. LNCS (Lecture Notes in Artificial Intelligence), vol. 1038, pp. pp. 42–55. Springer, Heidelberg (1996). https://doi.org/10.1007/BFb0031845
16. Rao, A.S., Georgeff, M.P.: BDI agents: from theory to practice. In: Proceeding of the International Conference on Multi-Agent Systems, pp. 312–319. San Francisco (1995)
17. Ricci, A., Piunti, M., Viroli, M., Omicini, A.: Environment programming in CArtAgO. In: Multi-Agent Programming: Languages, Tools and Applications, Chap. 8, pp. 259–288. Multiagent Systems, Artificial Societies, and Simulated Organizations, Springer, Boston (2009). https://doi.org/10.1007/978-0-387-89299-3_8
18. Smith, R.G.: The contract net protocol: high-level communication and control in a distributed problem solver. IEEE Trans. Comput. **29**(12), 1104–1113 (1980)

Distributed Decision-Making Based on Shared Knowledge in the Multi-Agent Programming Contest
"Dumping to Gather" Team Description

Christopher-Eyk Hrabia$^{(\boxtimes)}$, Marc Schmidt, Andrea Marie Weintraud, and Axel Hessler

Faculty of Electrical Engineering and Computer Science,
DAI-Labor, Technische Universität Berlin,
Ernst-Reuter-Platz 7, 10587 Berlin, Germany
christopher-eyk.hrabia@dai-labor.de

Abstract. The second Multi-Agent Programming Contest 2018 team of the Technische Universität Berlin results from the course *Applied Artificial Intelligence Project* that has taken place in the summer term 2018. The given target was to use our decision-making and planning framework ROS Hybrid Behaviour Planner (RHBP), which allows developing distributed multi-agent systems in the robotics domain. For the 2018 edition of the contest, the students particularly evaluated recently introduced features for knowledge sharing in RHBP. The united team for the official contest is formed by students from the course and their supervisors.

Keywords: Artificial Intelligence · Autonomous systems · Multi-Agent Programming · Decision-making · Planning · Knowledge sharing

1 Introduction

The participation of our team *Dumping to gather*[1] in the Multi-Agent Programming Contest (MAPC) is a follow-up of the approach that has been taken in the previous edition of the contest [1]. Our team is again the result of a Technische Universität Berlin (TUB) Master's program course (*Applied Artificial Intelligence Project*). Similarly, the final contest team is again formed by students (computer-science, business informatics and related fields) and their supervisors. During the execution of the project course, the students have been given the target to make use of the decision-making and planning framework ROS Hybrid Behaviour Planner (RHBP). RHBP allows to develop distributed multi-agent systems in the robotics domain. In the course itself we started with a simplified MAPC scenario only using 12 agents per team and reduced task complexity.

---

[1] Source code and documentation available: https://gitlab.tubit.tu-berlin.de/asp_b_ss18-group2/mapc_workspace.

© Springer Nature Switzerland AG 2019
T. Ahlbrecht et al. (Eds.): MAPC 2018, LNAI 11957, pp. 101–119, 2019.
https://doi.org/10.1007/978-3-030-37959-9_5

Later, the final solution of the course participants has been extended towards the contest implementation.

The requirement of using RHBP and how we executed the course is the same approach that we have used in the previous year [9], but as the framework RHBP has been further developed in the meanwhile, and we wanted to make use of the improved performance as well as recently introduced features. Particularly, the developed solution aimed to evaluate the applicability of knowledge sharing features that are now available in RHBP.

RHBP is a framework for decision-making and planning that especially targets the multi-robot domain [8,10]. RHBP allows to describe an agent declaratively in terms of its capabilities, like perception through sensors, behaviours for its actions, and conditions for specifying the outer boundary of the desired autonomous operation. Additionally, what the agents should aim for is controlled through the definition of goals. During runtime, RHBP uses a behaviour network approach for the short-term decision-making, which incorporates a state-based PDDL planner [15] for long-term considerations. Particularly, the PDDL planner is used as a guide for the short-term decision-making that is realised with the behaviour network. Additionally, the required domain and problem descriptions for the PDDL planner are automatically generated from RHBP behaviour models and fed into the planner. PDDL planning is not necessarily triggered on every decision-making step, instead, it is monitored when replanning is required, e.g. after goals have been achieved, added, and removed or if behaviours did not provide the expected influence on the world. The Behaviour network for opportunistic decision-making and the PDDL planner form together a hybrid architecture. Due to the fact that the behaviour models of RHBP do not include static transitions between the behaviours like for example required in hierarchical state machine or hierarchical task network approaches, it fosters adaptiveness and reconfigurability. Furthermore, RHBP is based on the Robot Operating System (ROS) [17] that is, despite its name, a Linux-based middleware for development, communication, and deployment of distributed systems.

In 2018, TUB also participated with another team (TUBDAI) that originated from a Master's thesis project supervised by the first author of this article. Both TUB teams shared a similar mission, they started from the same foundation with a given general infrastructure for communication and conversion of the simulation protocol based on our existing system from the 2017 contest edition, they are using RHBP, and are testing recently introduced features of the framework. However, both teams developed their solution independently, and we ensured that no details about their strategies and implementations have been exchanged. In consequence, we could observe that both teams opted for completely different strategies that also resulted in contrasting performances within the contest.

In the remainder of this article, we first introduce the new knowledge sharing features of RHBP in Sect. 2. Right after, our overall team strategy is described in Sect. 3. Subsequently, details about our application architecture and the declaratively implemented behaviour model are outlined in Sects. 4 and 5. An discussion of our results is presented in Sect. 6. Finally, we conclude with a summary of our insights and contributions as well as an outlook on future plans in Sect. 7.

2 Knowledge Base: Sharing Information in a Hybrid Behaviour Network

Missing points in existing behaviour network architectures and hybrid behaviour network approaches like [11,13,14] are concepts for information sharing amongst multiple entities. This is not surprising considering the fact that only [11] is targeting multi-agent systems. Nevertheless, a specific concept is also missing in the solution of [11] because the presented ABBA architecture is only providing the abstract concept of feature detectors. How individual agents exchange information is not considered.

The PDDL-based deliberative planning approaches [5,18] consider the problem of information sharing to some extent in their centralised solutions. ROSPlan from [5] uses a completely centralised approach with one central OWL knowledge base that has to be filled by the user of the framework based on a certain set of interfaces. The framework applies the interfaces to create an ontology that allows for determining when replanning is required. The SkiROS approach [18] has similarities to ROSPlan. It has also one central knowledge base, called World Model, but it partitions the knowledge into continuous, discrete, and semantic data. Nevertheless, neither ROSPlan nor SkiROS consider information sharing on an agent level, it functions only as a central input component for centralised planning.

In contrast to above described approaches, RHBP is also directly aiming for decentralised multi-robot systems, respectively multi-agent systems. In such cases, sharing information amongst agents can foster the cooperation and simplifies the creation of solutions for distributed problem solving, as shown in practice in [3]. As a consequence, it is crucial to allow for a straightforward implementation in RHBP, too. Examples for scenarios that require sharing information are, e.g. logistic scenarios as proposed by the MAPC but also general search and rescue or exploration scenarios, where the agents need to exchange information about which places have already been visited or which items have been found.

The solution from [3] is applying a blackboard architecture [7]. Despite its age, the blackboard architecture is still used [16,20] and provides a useful pattern for the implementation of adaptive intelligent systems. The basic idea behind a blackboard architecture is that a central knowledge base is periodically updated with knowledge from specialist agents that are having their own knowledge representations.

For RHBP, we followed the blackboard approach and integrated a component that is called *knowledge base*. The RHBP knowledge base allows to store arbitrary knowledge facts in a shared tuple space. Moreover, the implementation gives complete freedom of the instantiation. It is possible to have one central knowledge base, use individual knowledge bases per agent, or using different knowledge bases for certain agent groups. Likewise, an agent can also access to

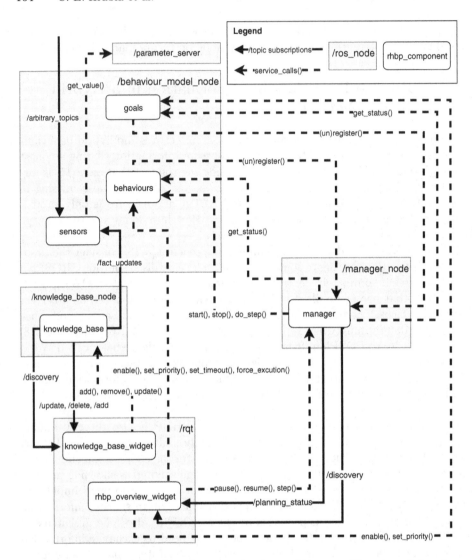

Fig. 1. RHBP core ROS node and communication architecture. Direction of the edges correspond to the initiated direction of the data flow.

several knowledge bases at the same time. From the implementation point of view, each knowledge base is a ROS node, which is identified by its name and namespace. All agents that know the name are able to store and retrieve information from the knowledge base. Furthermore, all knowledge bases are continuously broadcasting their name on a specific ROS topic for simplified discovery.

The implementation of the communication is also applying common ROS concepts such as the publish-subscribe pattern. This pattern is mainly chosen to implement filtering and notification of information. Here, the client agent is able to register a search pattern with placeholders for being updated in case desired tuples are updated, added, or deleted. The corresponding updates are shared over automatically created ROS topics. Here, a distinct topic for each type of changed information is created, which corresponds to one topic per pattern for: update, add, and delete. This becomes especially useful if multiple agents are interested in the same search pattern, which would be mapped to the same topics, allowing for notification broadcasts. The communication means are visualised in Fig. 1. All components of the RHBP are based on the ROS messaging architecture and are using ROS services and topics for communication.

On the client site of our knowledge base implementation, tuple facts can be stored in a local tuple cache to guarantee fast access to all required information. The local tuple cache is also beneficial in situations with interrupted communication and increases the robustness of the information exchange. All writing access is implemented with ROS services that are conveniently abstracted in an own knowledge base client library. The client library supports reading, writing, updating, and tuple existence checks. The tuple space implementation is based on the Linda tuple space [6] Python implementation *lindypy*[2], which has been further extended to enable additional search modes.

RHBP supports as well the information sharing through the ROS parameter server with specific behaviours and sensors for storing and retrieving information. This alternative solution can also be used to implement blackboard architectures. Nevertheless, the knowledge base implementation has the advantage of being much more efficient due to the publish-subscribe-patter. In order to access information from the parameter server, every information piece has to be polled. Furthermore, the parameter server is less flexible, only one central instance can be used, and it does not support filtering with search patterns.

The general knowledge base concept and implementation are entirely independent of RHBP and can also be used together with other ROS packages. For this reason, the implementation is also shipped as a separated ROS package. The RHBP integration is realised with specific classes in a RHBP extension package named *rhbp_utils*. This package includes special sensor and behaviour implementations for retrieving and manipulating knowledge in a knowledge base. This allows the direct integration of shared knowledge in the existing behaviour model concept with conditions and activators. The provided behaviour and sensor classes are also providing a base for application-specific implementations. Currently, the library contains a *KnowledgeUpdateBehaviour* that updates a certain fact once the behaviour has been activated, as well as various sensor implementation that allow to check for fact existence, retrieving specific facts matching a pattern or the number of matching facts.

Furthermore, the knowledge base implementation is accompanied by a GUI that allows to monitor, inspect, and manipulate the facts during execution. The GUI is implemented as a *rqt* plugin widget to conveniently integrate into the ROS ecosystem. *rqt* is a Qt-based framework for GUI development for ROS. It allows to freely configure combinations of visual widget plugins in a one or

---

[2] https://pypi.org/project/lindypy/.

many dockable windows. *rqt* is shipped with several included widget plugins and can be used to configure application specific monitoring and control GUIs. The knowledge base monitoring widget is illustrated in Fig. 2. The widget is implemented based on the described publish-subscribe pattern, too. Moreover, it also supports the configuration of patterns to filter the visualised information.

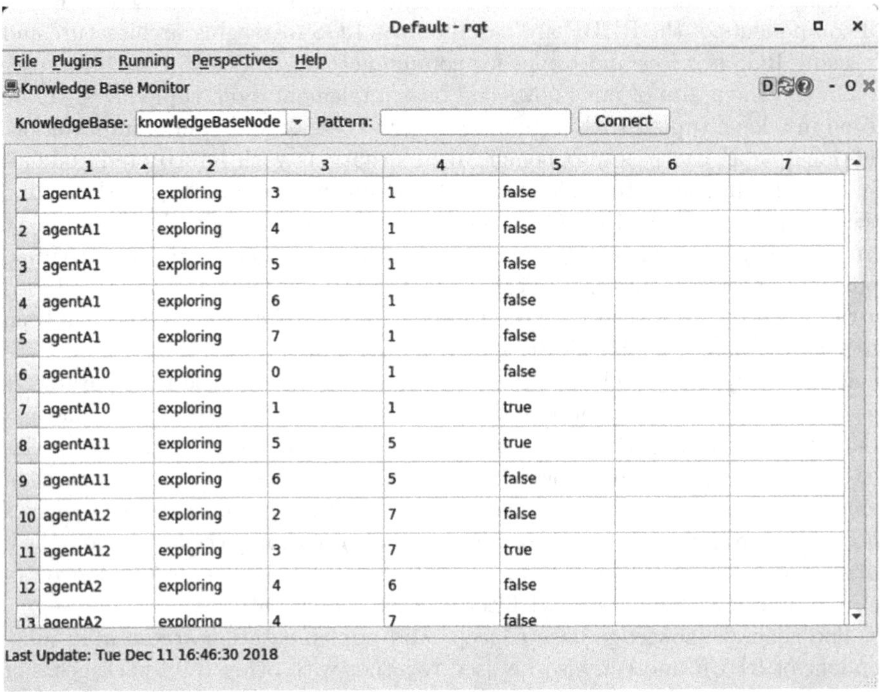
Default - rqt
File Plugins Running Perspectives Help
Knowledge Base Monitor
KnowledgeBase: knowledgeBaseNode
Pattern:
Connect
1 2 3 4 5 6 7
1 agentA1 exploring 3 1 false
2 agentA1 exploring 4 1 false
3 agentA1 exploring 5 1 false
4 agentA1 exploring 6 1 false
5 agentA1 exploring 7 1 false
6 agentA10 exploring 0 1 false
7 agentA10 exploring 1 1 true
8 agentA11 exploring 5 5 true
9 agentA11 exploring 6 5 false
10 agentA12 exploring 2 7 false
11 agentA12 exploring 3 7 true
12 agentA2 exploring 4 6 false
13 agentA2 exploring 4 7 false
Last Update: Tue Dec 11 16:46:30 2018

Fig. 2. Graphical knowledge base monitoring, inspection and control in ROS. Shown is a live view of the knowledge shared by our team.

All in all, the RHBP approach for knowledge sharing with the knowledge base component is modular in terms of distribution and decentralisation, tightly integrated into ROS and provides as the first behaviour-network based approach means for sharing knowledge over multiple agents running a behaviour model for task-level decision-making. Moreover, the knowledge base component allows to extend the basic behaviour network decision-making lifecycle of RHBP core, which is corresponding to the MAPE (monitor, analyse, plan, execute) loop concept, to the extended MAPE-K concept (monitor, analyse, plan, execute knowledge) [4,12]. Here, the monitoring is covered by the sensor components that provide the input for the system and the execution is realised by the specific behaviour implementation of the selected and executed behaviour. Whereas the actual decision-making is realised with the behaviour network implementation that resemble the stages analyse and plan of MAPE. In the MAPE-K concept, a knowledge component is required and is used to share data amongst the monitor, analyse, plan and execution components. In this respect, the presented knowledge base integration concept is exactly enabling the proposed process where the monitoring components create the knowledge, which corresponds to the knowledge sensors in RHBP. Later in the lifecycle, other RHBP components like the behaviours as execution component are also able to modify the stored knowledge.

3   MAPC Strategy

The strategy of our team *Dumping to gather* is team-oriented where all agents are able to do all types of tasks and independently choose amongst them while cooperating in order to prevent redundant work. In this respect, all agents are responsible for exploration and resource gathering.

The implemented main strategy followed the RHBP approach of 2017 with on demand job processing and item gathering. The implementation is addressing all job types except for auction jobs. Additionally, the newly required well building is also executed on-demand if sufficient money is available.

In general, all agents share information about items, facilities, wells, agents, and visited grid points with each other. The sharing of all permanent information is comprehensibly making use of the RHBP knowledge base component that we have introduced in the previous section. All non-persistent information is shared through dedicated ROS topics in a broadcast-like manner, which is the case for all information that is automatically updated every simulation step by the MASSim simulation server.

For the implementation of the exploration, the simulation map area is partitioned into grid cells reflecting the cell size of the simulation. The coordination of the exploration is implicit: Already visited grid cells are being shared amongst the agents through the knowledge base so that each agent can choose a not yet visited point. Here, the agents are choosing the closest not yet visited cell until all resource nodes have been discovered. However, this implicit self-organised exploration is a custom scenario specific implementation that does not apply the existing self-organisation extension of RHBP [8], which would have potentially simplified the realisation of a self-organisation mechanism.

Furthermore, the new MAPC 2018 scenario features upgrades and selling of item is not used because upgrades seemed too expensive in comparison to the money required for building wells and selling items was also considered as less beneficial in comparison to fulfilling entire jobs.

To coordinate the job fulfilment we use a contract-net-based protocol [19] that enables decentralised coordination. For this reason, each agent has an auctioneer node, which is responsible for managing the auctioning process amongst the agents, and a bidder node, which selects and bids for a sub-task. Every incoming job is assigned to an auctioneer node in a round-robin fashion. The auction is done in stages. First, the job is decomposed into different tasks according to the items and required capacity. It is possible that the tasks are linked since they can depend on a preceding task. For example, if one task contains the gathering of an item, and another task contains the delivery of that item to a store, both tasks should be operated by the same agent. The auctioneer node decomposes the job and publishes the sub-tasks. Secondly, the bidder nodes of the agents decide if they are able to do a sub-task by considering their load, the task's time restrictions and their already assigned plans and bid for the task with the corresponding computed plan. Selecting a bid is done by choosing the plan that will be finished first in simulation step time. In case a job cannot be finished in time, all unused items are stored in storages and later reused.

The agents are mostly autonomous without any central decision-making. Although the agents rely on the auctioneer nodes of the other agents to publish sub-tasks and coordinate the internal auctions, the system is resilient against failures of individuals due to the round-robin assignment of the job coordinating agent as described before. In the worst case of a malfunctional or not responding coordinating agent, the coordination would just fail for one simulation step and continued in the next step with the next agent.

If an agent is not executing a sub-task of a delivery job, it is having some idle time. If that is the case, the agents have the following priorities: First, fulfilling jobs, secondly, building wells if sufficient money is available, thirdly dismantling wells of opponents and lastly exploring the environment. In addition, exploration is done by all agents at the beginning of all simulations to discover all resource nodes that are required to assemble items. Well construction is done in a group of agents to speed up the construction process. The build-up wells are positioned around the border of the simulation map to minimise the probability of accidental discovery by the opponent because the borders are not visited without explicit exploration order.

All in all, the strategy aims for a distributed solution with autonomous decision-making of every agent without relying on particular roles for individual agents.

4   Application Architecture

The implemented general application architecture is very similar to the agent architecture of 2017 [9] but it is extended with separated ROS nodes for initiating and participating in auctions used for the contract-net-based coordination. The diagram in Fig. 3 shows the multi-agent system architecture.

A more detailed architecture and data flow between the particular sub-components within an individual agent is visualised in Fig. 4. Generally, the system consists of the following components:

- MASSim Simulation Server
- MacRosBridge
- Agent Node
- Auctioneer Node
- Bidder Node
- GraphHopperProcessHandler

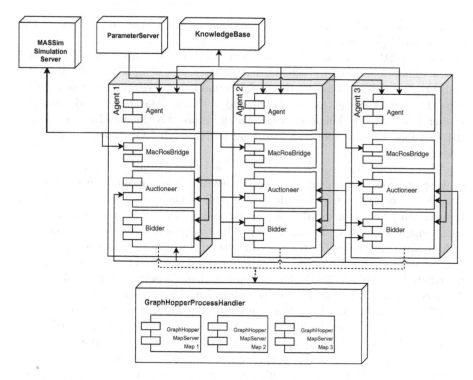

Fig. 3. Multi-agent system architecture and data flow between ROS nodes (processes) for three agents. Different line styles are only used for visibility. Arrows indicate direction of data flow.

Moreover, we see the knowledge sharing infrastructure is only used on the inter-agent level, while the intra-agent communication relies completely on common ROS communication means. The RHBP knowledge base is used to store all information that has to be persistent, in particular we store exploration grid points, discovered resources, and found opponent wells. The ParameterServer is only used to retrieve some static configurations after the system is initialised.

Graphhopper is the routing library that is used to determine distance on the map, which is also applied internally by the MASSim Simulation Server [2]. For each simulation map a separate GraphHopperMapServer with the corresponding map data is started on a different port, while the management and coordination is transparently managed by the GraphHopperProcessHandler.

The MASSim Simulation Server is sending and receiving the information of the simulation to the MacRosBridge using a XML protocol and a socket interface. Subsequently, the MacRosBridge can forward the information of the simulation to the Agent Node. The Agent, which also contains a RHBPAgent component, has an Agent that receives the information from the MacRosBridge. In turn the Agent put the information it gained from the MacRosBridge into the Perception Management. The perception of the world is also associated to the RHBPAgent, the Auctioneer and the Bidder, so all component of an agent have access to the current world perception.

The RHBP Agent is the component used for the operational planning and decision-making of the agents, particularly, the component initialises the behaviour model and triggers the decision-making lifecycle in every simulation step. The world perception is also shared with the Auctioneer Node and the Bidder Node by the MacRosBridge. Furthermore, the MacRosBridge informs the Auctioneer Node about an incoming job through ROS topic-based broadcasts.

As we already described, the coordination of incoming jobs is done with a contract-net-based approach. Here, every agent can be an auctioneer. By using the IDs of both the agent and the job as well as the overall amount of agents, the auctioneer is determined in a round robin manner. This prevents that one agent might always be the auctioneer. The components Auctioneer Node and Bidder Node are needed for the coordination of the agents. As stated before, the auctioneer receives information about an incoming job from the world perception distributed by the MacRosBridge. The job is then decomposed into tasks in the Job Decomposer. The tasks are then assigned in the auction.

When a Bidder Node receives the task from an Auction, it elaborates an operation plan using its TaskHandler. The operational plan considers the route each agent has to traverse in order to complete certain tasks. For this reason the TaskHandler makes use of the Graphhopper Routing component.

Subsequently, the operational plan is used as a bid for the auction. The Auctioneer chooses the bidder whose plan has the lowest end step. Sometimes the duration of another plan might be shorter. However, it must be considered, that the agent with the shortest duration could be busy. Hence, the agent might finish later even though the duration of the task is shorter. Therefore, the lowest end step is chosen. Once the bidder is assigned to a task by the Auctioneer, the assignment must be acknowledged by the bidder. When this is done, the assignment is given to the Plan-Handler. The assigned plans are given to RHBPAgent in the Agent Node. Then RHBP is used to execute the operational decision-making that addresses the given plan by selecting appropriate behaviours. Executed behaviours result in an action which is returned to the MacRosBridge. In turn, the MacRosBridge forwards each action to the Simulation Server so it can be processed.

5   Behaviour Model

During the contest preparation the team developed an own implementation pattern for RHBP that is called *BehaviourGraph*. A *BehaviourGraph* is an abstract component that is used to group certain behaviours, sensors, conditions and goals of a higher level task. In contrast to the NetworkBehaviour, which are applied by the TUBDAI implementation, the *BehaviourGraphs* are not adding additional decision-making layers, all behaviours and goals are still registered to the same RHBP manager. *BehaviourGraphs* are used only for providing convenience

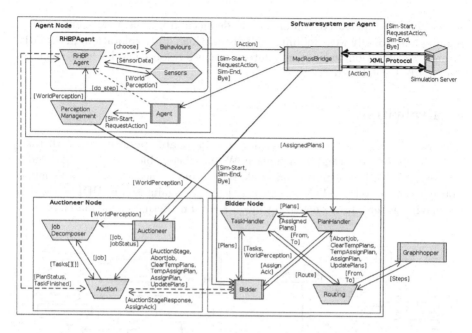

Fig. 4. System architecture and data flow between the sub-components of one agent, which is not considering the knowledge sharing amongst multiple agents.

functions for common initialisations, updating knowledge, adding preconditions to all contained behaviours, resetting, as well as task-specific functionalities. *BehaviourGraphs* particularly simplify modelling by avoiding repeated condition assignments.

The implemented behaviour model used for decision-making is visualised in Fig. 5. The behaviour model diagram is a modelling language, respectively notation, which we developed ourselves to visualise the relationship between the first level components of a RHBP behaviour model. It was introduced in [9] due to the reason that existing languages, such as Business Process Model and Notation (BPMN) or Unified Modelling Language (UML), could not reflect non-sequential precondition, action, and effect relationships. Notably, the conditions modelled for the *BehaviourGraphs* are reflecting the aforementioned main priorities of the agents. Each main task is modelled in one *BehaviourGraph*. The implementation of the job fulfilment and related coordination, see lower left *BehaviourGraph*, is integrated similarly to the implementation of TUBDAI 2017. Here, the actual job tasks are determined by the RHBP-independent coordinator and then operated by the multi-purpose execute_plan and finish_plan behaviour. The comparison between the model of "Dumping to gather" in Fig. 5 and the previous version of TUBDAI 2017 in [9] is also visualising the increased complexity of the model with more behaviours, conditions, and goals. In detail, the old TUBDAI model contained only 5 behaviours and 2 goals, whereas we have 5 *BehaviourGraphs* with all in all 5 goals and 13 behaviours. Nevertheless, a detailed comparison shows that the increased complexity is deduced from the new scenario that requires additionally well-building, well dismantling, and exploration. In the 2017 scenario, exploration was not mandatory because resource nodes have not been required to assemble items.

6   Evaluation

Our team "Dumping to gather" achieved a reasonable performance with their implementation, resulting in a 4th place. We have been able to address all mandatory elements of the scenario and made points and gained money in all simulation matches, see Table 1. We gained a clear win against team UDESC, which was having general problems with timeouts etc. Furthermore, the match against

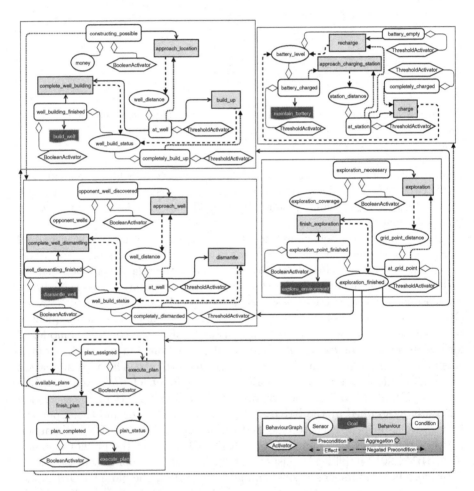

Fig. 5. Behaviour model for agent task execution of *Dumping to gather*. *Behaviour-Graphs* are containers to apply conditions to multiple behaviours.

Table 1. MAPC 2018 simulation match results of Dumping to gather. Rating: 3 score points per won simulation. 1 score point for a draw.

Match	Sim 1	Sim 2	Sim 3	Score
Akuanduba-UDESC vs. Dumping to gather	130 : 6402	0 : 18677	0 : 16936	0:9
Dumping to gather vs. Jason-DTU	3030 : 3472	9973 : 14332	5847 : 8545	0:9
Dumping to gather vs. Smart_JaCaMo	2303 : 4581	9163 : 62413	4367 : 29543	0:9
Dumping to gather vs. TUBDAI	216 : 11404	1192 : 25954	798 : 5577	0:9

Jason-DTU has been very close and counterbalanced but was barely lost. The other two matches against the two best teams of TUBDAI and Smart_JaCaMo have been lost more clearly.

7   Conclusion

In this article, we described how a coordination of a multi-agent team in the complex scenario of the MAPC can be realised on the foundation of the decision-making and planning framework RHBP and the underlying communication infrastructure of ROS. Particularly, we have used our participation in the contest to evaluate certain knowledge sharing features that have been introduced recently into the RHBP framework. We did not gain special insights about if this approach was optimal or not as our team strategy focused on the wrong aspects of the scenario. Nevertheless, we have been able to obtain a feasibility proof of the application of our knowledge base feature in a complex multi-agent scenario. Finally, our team was able to keep up with the other teams in general.

In the future we would like to evaluate another new feature of RHBP that was not finalised at the time of the contest. The new feature is a delegation component that allows applying automated delegation of tasks including decomposition and allocation of tasks within a group of multiple agents. This component allows to increase the decoupling of task delegations in hierarchical decision models to foster the flexibility and adaptation means.

1   Team Overview: Short Answers

1.1   Participants and Their Background

What was your motivation to participate in the contest?
  - The motivation for the participation is twofold. First, we wanted to further evaluate the performance of the RHBP framework within a complex scenario testing certain features. Secondly, students are introduced in the framework and try to apply it to the challenging scenario.

What is the history of your group? (course project, thesis, ...)

- Researchers of the DAI-Labor started to participate in the contest in 2007. Since then they have contributed to every edition of the contest and have won four of them using successive generations of the JIAC multi-agent framework. Our current team originates from the supervisors and two volunteering students from the "Applied Artificial Intelligence Project" summer term 2018 course of the Technische Universität Berlin. The applied framework RHBP is developed in one Ph.D. thesis and several independent Bachelor and Master's theses.

What is your field of research? Which work therein is related?

- Our field of research is multi-agent systems applied in the robotics domain.

1.2   Development

How much time did you invest in the contest for programming vs. other tasks (for example organization)? creating vs. optimizing your agents?

- We spend approximately 300 h on the scenario-specific programming and 40 h on the team coordination and contest registration. Moreover, we have done almost no optimisation due to the fact that we still finalised foundational functionality until the contest started.

How many lines of code did you produce for your final agent team?

- 8600

How many people were involved and to which degree?

- *Christopher-Eyk Hrabia* (PhD Student at Technische Universität Berlin) - Supervision, technical consulting, RHBP improvements, MAPC communication infrastructure
- *Marc Schmidt and Marie Weintraud* (MSc Students at Technische Universität Berlin) - Implementation of everything MAPC 2018 scenario specific like agent behaviour and strategy development.
- *Axel Hessler* (Post-Doc at Technische Universität Berlin) was responsible for the infrastructure and overall administration.

When did you start working on your agents?

- Mid April 2018 (begin summer term)

1.3   System Details

How do your agents work together? (coordination, information sharing, ...)

- All information is shared amongst the agents. Information sharing differentiates in information that has to be persisted and information that is automatically updates and provided by the simulation server.
- For each job one agent takes responsibility and coordinates the task decomposition and allocation with a contract net protocol.

What are critical components of your team?
- Our most critical components are the special ROS nodes implemented to exhibit the contract net protocol, namely the auctioneer and bidder. Furthermore, the new development pattern BehaviourGraphs for RHBP has also been critical for the executability of our team.

Can your agents change their behaviour during runtime? If so, what triggers the changes?
- No, but our agents adjust their behaviour based on the selected behaviour implementations, which is selected through decision-making and planning of RHBP.

Did you have to make changes to the team (e.g. fix critical bugs) during the contest?
- Yes, we did not consider to have that many wells and needed to bugfix our code to be able to create more wells. The reason for this was that in the contest setup all jobs allowed to gain considerable more money in comparison to the sample configuration, shared before the contest, which made building wells much easier.

How do you organize your agents? Do you use e.g. hierarchies? Is your organization implicit or explicit?
- We have an explicit organisation through contract-net protocol for the job fulfilment.
- The auctioning agent (job responsible agent) is selected round robin based on the job-id.
- Drones are responsible for exploration after an initial exploration stage where all agents are implicitly coordinated exploring the map
- In general, all agents are allowed to fulfill all tasks

Is most of your agents' behavior emergent on an individual or team level?
- We apply a hybrid planning and decision making framework (RHBP - ROS Hybrid Behaviour Planner) for the execution of the agent behaviours. This results in adaptive and reactive behaviour for individual agents, based on the current perception. But the deliberative part still tries to optimize/plan for shortest routes and resource management as charging. All in all this might lead to emergent behaviour on individual and team level.

If your agents perform some planning, how many steps do they plan ahead?
- Agent plan ahead as far as possible to determine if a job can be completed within one simulation (max. 1000steps)
- RHBP planner has a configurable limit for planning steps, here 1000 steps.

If you have a perceive-think-act cycle, how is it synchronized with the server?
- The decision-making and planning cycle, which we consider the "think", is initially triggered by the "request action" ("perceive") from the server for each agent. If answering a request action takes too long the agents are dropping the request and are starting over with the most recent request.

How did you go about debugging your system?
- We have not used special tools besides RHBP rqt plugings. In general we applied manual logging and stepwise debugging with PyCharm.

Which operating system did you use, and is your team portable to other operating systems?
- Ubuntu 16.04 - Everything (every Linux) that supports ROS will work.

What hardware did you use to run your agent team? (RAM, CPU, disk space, multiple computers, any other notable requirements)
- Virtual Machine with 32 GB RAM, 4 Cores Intel(R) Xeon(R) CPU E5-2697A v4 @2.60 GHz, no special hard-disk.

1.4   Scenario and Strategy

What is the main strategy of your agent team? Our strategy is based on the following parts.
- Exploration with drones
- If jobs can be fulfilled they are targeted with highest priority.
- If no job is in queue and enough money for well building is available, wells are build
- If neither jobs are targeted or wells are built, opponent wells are attacked
- In all other cases the agents are randomly exploring the resource nodes and already build wells.

How do your agents decide which jobs to complete?
- Only mission jobs and priced jobs are addressed.
- We do not have a cost-benefit analysis, we try to complete jobs in the order they appear.
- If jobs can be completed in time they are processed

Do you have different strategies for the different roles?
- Partially yes, in our strategy drones are responsible for exploration but in general everything else is done by all agents.

Do your agents form ad-hoc teams to complete a task?
- No, all job completion is pre-planned by the coordination agents.

How do your agents decide when and where to build wells?
- The selected position depends on the location of the agent. Building takes place if enough money is available and no other job tasks are due, see above.

If your agents accumulated a lot of currency, why did they not spend it immediately?
- The reason is that our solutions puts highest priority on job completion, this can potentially result in an accumulation of money .

1.5   And the Moral of It Is ...

What did you learn from participating in the contest?
- Focusing on strategic aspects would have improved the result.
- The sample scenarios have been much more difficult than the final contest configurations, which made it difficult to configure our agents appropriately.
- We should focus less on job completion because it was not as crucial as expected.
- Effective well building/dismantling showed out to be more important.

What are the strong and weak points of your team?
- Strong: job completion
- Weak: We have not been able to implement a cost-benefit analysis of jobs and our behaviour model is rigid not providing enough freedom for adaptation.

How viable were your chosen programming language, methodology, tools, and algorithms?
- The chosen approach with Python, ROS, RHBP was suitable and performed well in our opinion.

Did you encounter new problems during the contest?
- Yes, we pre-planned to less possible well building locations (we build around the border of the map)

Did playing against other agent teams bring about new insights on your own agents?
- Yes, our job execution performed well, but the locations for well building was not well chosen and leaded to long travel times for the agents.

What would you improve if you wanted to participate in the same contest a week from now (or next year)?
- We would put less priority on job completion and concentrate on more effective well building.

Which aspect of your team cost you the most time?
- Understanding this question as time of steps in the matches. Our agents spend most time for the on demand job completion as well as time for travelling between the well building locations.

Why did your team perform as it did? Why did the other teams perform better/worse than you did?
- Because we focused to much on fulfilling the scenario of the contest instead of developing a unique strategy.

1.6   The Future of the MAPC

What can be improved regarding the contest for next year?
- Providing similar preconditions for all participants: Hardware limitations, connection, match appointments.

What kind of scenario would you like to play next? What kind of features should the new scenario have?

- It would be interesting to have the possibility of eliminating opponent agents as well as a dynamic agent creation and not a fixed amount of agents.
- The sample configuration should be closer to the actual contest configuration to allow for selecting the strategy more effectively.

Should the teams be allowed to make changes to their agents during the contest (even based on opponent agent behaviour observed in earlier matches)? If yes, should only some changes be legal and which ones (e.g. bugfixes), and how to decide a change's classification? If no, should we ensure that no changes are made and how?

- No, all used code should be submitted before the contest. Nevertheless, bugfixes could be allowed through reviewed pull requests.

Do you have ideas to reduce the impact of unforeseen strategies (e.g., playing a second leg after some time)?

- Everything that is not exploiting bugs in the simulation and is possible with the given API should be allowed. Unforeseen strategies should be encouraged to make the contest more interesting. The challenge should be to create autonomous agents that are performing well also in unexpected situations.

References

1. Ahlbrecht, T., Dix, J., Fiekas, N.: Multi-agent programming contest 2017. Ann. Math. Artif. Intell. **84**(1), 1–16 (2018)
2. Ahlbrecht, T., Dix, J., Schlesinger, F.: From testing agent systems to a scalable simulation platform. In: Eiter, T., Strass, H., Truszczyński, M., Woltran, S. (eds.) Advances in Knowledge Representation, Logic Programming, and Abstract Argumentation. LNCS (LNAI), vol. 9060, pp. 47–62. Springer, Cham (2015). https://doi.org/10.1007/978-3-319-14726-0_4
3. Albayrak, S., Krallmann, H.: Verteilte kooperierende wissensbasierte systeme in der fertigungssteuerung. In: Görke, W., Rininsland, H., Syrbe, M. (eds.) Information als Produktionsfaktor, pp. 564–576. Springer, Heidelberg (1992). https://doi.org/10.1007/978-3-642-77810-0_52
4. Brun, Y., et al.: Engineering self-adaptive systems through feedback loops. In: Cheng, B.H.C., de Lemos, R., Giese, H., Inverardi, P., Magee, J. (eds.) Software Engineering for Self-Adaptive Systems. LNCS, vol. 5525, pp. 48–70. Springer, Heidelberg (2009). https://doi.org/10.1007/978-3-642-02161-9_3
5. Cashmore, M., et al.: ROSPlan: planning in the robot operating system. In: Proceedings International Conference on Automated Planning and Scheduling, ICAPS, pp. 333–341 (2015)
6. Gelernter, D., Carriero, N., Chandran, S.: Parallel programming in Linda. Yale University. Department of Computer Science (1985)
7. Hayes-Roth, B.: A blackboard architecture for control. Artif. Intell. **26**(3), 251–321 (1985)
8. Hrabia, C.-E., Kaiser, T.K., Albayrak, S.: Combining self-organisation with decision-making and planning. In: Belardinelli, F., Argente, E. (eds.) EUMAS/AT -2017. LNCS (LNAI), vol. 10767, pp. 385–399. Springer, Cham (2018). https://doi.org/10.1007/978-3-030-01713-2_27

9. Hrabia, C.-E., Lehmann, P.M., Battjbuer, N., Hessler, A., Albayrak, S.: Applying robotic frameworks in a simulated multi-agent contest. Ann. Math. Artif. Intell. **84**, 117–138 (2018)
10. Hrabia, C.-E., Wypler, S., Albayrak, S.: Towards goal-driven behaviour control of multi-robot systems. In: 2017 3rd International Conference on Control, Automation and Robotics (ICCAR), pp. 166–173, April 2017
11. Jung, D.: An architecture for cooperation among autonomous agents (1998)
12. Kephart, J.O., Chess, D.M.: The vision of autonomic computing. Computer **36**(1), 41–50 (2003)
13. Lee, Y.-S., Cho, S.-B.: A hybrid system of hierarchical planning of behaviour selection networks for mobile robot control. Int. J. Adv. Robot. Syst. **11**(4), 1–13 (2014)
14. Maes, P.: How to do the right thing. Connect. Sci. **1**(3), 291–323 (1989)
15. Mcdermott, D., et al.: PDDL - The Planning Domain Definition Language (1998)
16. Perico, D.H., et al.: Humanoid robot framework for research on cognitive robotics. J. Control Autom. Electr. Syst. **29**(4), 470–479 (2018)
17. Quigley, M., et al.: ROS: an open-source robot operating system. In: ICRA Workshop on Open Source Software, vol. 3, no. 3.2, p. 5 (2009)
18. Rovida, F., et al.: SkiROS—a skill-based robot control platform on top of ROS. In: Koubaa, A. (ed.) Robot Operating System (ROS). SCI, vol. 707, pp. 121–160. Springer, Cham (2017). https://doi.org/10.1007/978-3-319-54927-9_4
19. Smith, R.G.: The contract net protocol: high-level communication and control in a distributed problem solver. IEEE Trans. Comput. **12**, 1104–1113 (1980)
20. Tzafestas, S.G.: Mobile robot control and navigation: a global overview. J. Intell. Robot. Syst. **91**, 35–58 (2018)

ROS Hybrid Behaviour Planner: Behaviour Hierarchies and Self-organisation in the Multi-Agent Programming Contest
TUBDAI Team Description Multi-Agent Programming Contest 2018

Christopher-Eyk Hrabia$^{(\boxtimes)}$, Michael Franz Ettlinger, and Axel Hessler

Faculty of Electrical Engineering and Computer Science,
DAI-Labor, Technische Universität Berlin,
Ernst-Reuter-Platz 7, 10587 Berlin, Germany
christopher-eyk.hrabia@dai-labor.de

Abstract. While the decision-making and planning framework ROS Hybrid Behaviour Planner (RHBP) has been used in a wide variety of projects, newer features have not yet been tested in complex scenarios. One of those features allows creating multiple independent levels of decision-making by encapsulating a separate behaviour network into behaviours. Another one is an extension for implicit coordination through self-organisation. This paper discusses our system that was developed for the multi-agent contest 2018 using RHBP, while especially making use of newer features wherever possible. Our team TUBDAI achieved the shared top spot in the contest, showing that RHBP and in particular the new features can be used successfully in a complex scenario and measures up to the multi-agent frameworks, other teams have used. Especially, when a last-minute change to the contest environment required us to integrate substantial strategy changes in last-minute, it turned out that RHBP fostered adaptiveness during our development.

Keywords: Artificial Intelligence · Autonomous systems · Multi-agent programming · Decision-making · Planning · Self-organisation

1 Introduction

The multi-agent programming contest (MAPC) provides a testbed for evaluating multi-agent research results in an applied and competitive setting since many years. Participating in the contest has long tradition at Technische Universität Berlin (TUB) (e.g. [4–6]). The motivation for participation in the contest was always twofold. First, to use it as a platform to evaluate our multi-agent frameworks in complex multi-agent problems of the contest. Secondly, to use the competition setting as a platform for introducing our research to new users like

T. Ahlbrecht et al. (Eds.): MAPC 2018, LNAI 11957, pp. 120–143, 2019.
https://doi.org/10.1007/978-3-030-37959-9_6

students, which apply our frameworks either in their thesis projects or project courses. In 2017, we have introduced the framework ROS Hybrid Behaviour Planner (RHBP) [11] for the realisation of our contest team [10], which has its roots in the robotics domain.

In particular, RHBP is applied for the implementation of the individual task-level decision-making and planning of the agents as well as the coordination amongst the agents. RHBP is targeting the multi-robot domain and is based on the Robot Operating System (ROS) [17] framework that provides means for deployment, decentralised execution, and communication. The RHBP combines the advantages of reactive opportunistic decision-making and goal-oriented proactive planning in a modular hybrid architecture. Decision-making is based on behaviour networks [14] that allow for dynamic state transitions and the definition of goals, while the deliberative part is realised on the foundation of the Planning Domain Description Language (PDDL) [15] and the particular planner Metric-FF [7].

The reason for evaluating RHBP in a simulated comparable abstract multi-agent scenario instead to real robot applications is that real robot applications require to address a huge overhead of other domain-specific challenges, such as hardware failures, very uncertain environments, and difficulties in basic robotic capabilities like object detection and localisation [8]. Due to the reason that RHBP is a generic framework for decision-making, planning and coordination of multi-robot systems the evaluation in the MAPC, which focuses on task-level agent control, allows us to concentrate on these research aspects.

Since 2016 the contest scenario has been using the discrete and distributed last-mile delivery simulation (MASSim) [2] on top of geographic map data from different real cities (*OpenStreetMap* data). The simulation allows competition of several teams consisting of independent agents. Delivery jobs are randomly generated and split into three categories: *Mission jobs* are compulsorily assigned, *auction jobs* are assigned by prior auction and *regular jobs* are open to everyone. Jobs are monetarily rewarded on fulfilment and can only be accomplished once. Moreover, jobs consist of several items which can be purchased at shops (2016–2017) or gathered in resource nodes (2017–2018), as well as stored in warehouses. Furthermore, the 2018 edition of the contest scenario was extended with the obligation of building wells to generate score points required to win matches. Building wells required money that is earned by completing delivery jobs or selling resource items in a shop. The well-building extension in 2018 fosters more interaction and direct competition between the teams aside from increasing the overall search space for finding the most optimal solution. Moreover, the number of used agents per team was increased from 28 to 34 agents.

In the 2018 participation, the goal of our team was to evaluate more recent features of RHBP that have not been tested before in a complex application. Team TUBDAI focuses on two features in particular. First, so-called *Network-Behaviours* that allow creating multiple independent levels of decision-making by encapsulating a separate behaviour network into behaviours of the behaviour network model of RHBP. Secondly, the extension *so_data* for implicit coordination through self-organisation [9]. The extension *so_data* incorporates the concept of a virtual gradient space as a common data structure and communication mean for various self-organisation patterns. Additionally, the *so_data* package already contains several abstract implementations of self-organisation patterns, while the particular integration with RHBP is enabled through the package *rhbp_selforga*, which contains special sensor and behaviour components.

The participants of the 2018 edition of the contest consisted of five international teams, with two independent participations from TUB, namely *TUBDAI* and *Dumping to Gather*. Both teams from TUB are applying a RHBP-based implementation as a follow-up of the introduction of RHBP in the 2017 contest [10]. However, both teams did only share the starting point with general components developed in the year before, like the protocol proxy mac_ros_bridge and the integration of the routing library GraphHopper. Despite these general components, both teams developed their solution completely from scratch, which resulted in two very different general strategies. Both teams have been supported by the technical supervision of the first author of this article. Nevertheless, strategic decisions or implementations were never communicated or shared between both teams. The resulting implementations are both highly decentralised with all agents taking operational decisions autonomously using RHBP behaviour models. Only the evaluation of published delivery jobs is done in centralised components in both cases. Moreover, both teams apply an own contract-net based implementation for the coordination of the assembly and delivery for fulfilling the jobs.

The remainder of the paper is structured as follows. In the Sect. 2, we analyse and summarise the particular challenges of the MAPC 2018 for our team. Next, Sect. 3 outlines and describes our general team strategy, whereas Sects. 4 and 5 provide details about our implemented architecture and coordination approach. Subsequently, Sect. 6 describes the behaviour model we have implemented for the autonomous decision-making of our agents making use of our RHBP framework. In Sect. 7 we describe and discuss our contest results based on statistics and observations we made in the individual matches. Finally, Sect. 8 concludes this work with a summary of the contributions as well as emphasising future steps we plan to address.

2   MAPC 2018 Challenges

The complex contest scenario offers a comprehensive environment to design, implement and evaluate a multi-agent system. This results in some unique challenges which are covered in this section.

In the last two years, cooperation between agents became a bigger focus of the contest. While in preceding scenarios, it was possible to develop viable solutions without cooperation between agents by letting each agent independently work on parts of the problem, now there are key actions that require cooperation between multiple agents [1]. In this year, jobs only use items which need to be assembled first, requiring the implementation of complex cooperation and communication between agents.

Some environmental parameters are generated randomly, which results in much variation between simulations, thus making it harder to develop a solution that can work well with different configurations. The number of possible finished products to build can vary quite substantially between simulations. Strategies like proactively assembling and hoarding items work best with a few finished products, while a higher number of finished products makes just-in-time gathering, assembly and delivery more efficient. The maps differ in size and street layout, therefore changing the necessary effort for discovery as well as the effectiveness of different agent roles. These and other differences in the unknown contest configuration make it harder for teams to develop solutions that work well in all cases.

Following [12] the characteristics of multi-agent systems are having incomplete information or capabilities, no global system control, decentralised data, and asynchronous computation. In that spirit, a primary goal of participating in a multi-agent contest should be to develop a decentralised solution. Nevertheless, some previous submissions had shared data structures between agents and used a central planner, which decided on actions for all agents. The individual agents were then only responsible for making sure that enough battery is available to perform those predefined actions. The benefit of such systems is that they are easier to implement, as not much effort has to be put into agent communication and coordination. Furthermore, the effectiveness of such systems can be observed for example with last year's winning submission by BusyBeaver [16]. However, our goal was to decentralise as many decisions as possible, letting each agent autonomously decide what to do next, except on those few cases where this is impossible (e.g. job execution). Moreover, this decentralised approach allows that each agent could potentially be run on a different machine.

Another challenge is the large number of possible options for strategy decisions. The diversity in facilities and actions allow for many different strategies. It would take a massive development effort to make use of all available facilities and actions, so it is necessary to evaluate options and implement only the most promising ones.

During each simulation, a team has to compete against another team on the same map, which results in unique challenges. Regular job rewards are only awarded to the team, who can perform the job faster, therefore making job delivery speed a major design goal. The competitive setting also requires weighting actions of increasing one's own score with actions to decrease the opponents' score. Also, because of the broad spectrum of available strategies, it is harder to design a system, that performs well against varying opposing strategies.

One limitation imposed by the contest is that actions have to be submitted at latest four seconds after a step percept is published. Due to the limited timeframe, it is hard to find the optimal solution and a compromise has to be found between an ideal decision-making process and one, that can be finished quickly.

3 Strategy

The main strategy of the TUBDAI implementation is a stockpile with feedback strategy. Here, it is the goal to gather resources, assemble items in advance, and fulfil jobs that can be performed with the available item stock. First, the agents explore the environment until a resource node for each base item is discovered. Then all agents start to gather resources to achieve a stock of base items depending on the assigned priority for further assembly. Agent groups are formed dynamically to assemble items once the agent capacity is exceeded. The jobs are then prioritised according to a calculated reward. The reward is given by a ratio of required work and revenue. If a job reaches the defined reward threshold and all items of the job are currently in stock, the job is executed. Furthermore, urgent item demands such as induced by mission jobs, which would result in fines if not fulfilled, are also considered on demand based on feedback from other higher-level components like the job planner by dynamically adjusting the priorities of the respective items. The feedback allows reacting and changing the priorities of finished products and base items, which results in better adaptability to changes on demand, while still maintaining the efficiency of a general stockpile strategy. The advantage of this stockpile with feedback strategy is a fast job performance, enabling decentralised decision-making by individual agents to avoid a single point of failure, while also enabling on-demand execution based on the priority feedback. A disadvantage is that assembled finished products may not match any job and cannot be used, hence potentially wasting time resources.

Even though we aimed for a decentralised solution, the rating of jobs is centralised in one agent for simplification because there is no difference in between the job perception amongst the agents and the cost-benefit analysis is as well agent independent. The distribution of task from the decomposed jobs is then realised using a contract net protocol [19] involving all agents in a decentralised and distributed fashion. All other components are completely decentralised, too. Each agent has its own RHBP-based decision-making and planning component.

For the execution of jobs, an algorithm involving a chain of decisions has been developed. At the end of the chain, the scenario-specific job planner inspects which items currently provide high money returns. This information is converted into a finished product prioritisation. This prioritisation is then used by the next link in the decision chain, the assembly decision. The agents always decide autonomously which items should be assembled next and share their decision with the others. This decision is mainly based on what is needed for job execution as well as on the available items, and the finished products that are already assembled. In turn, this decision creates a prioritisation of base items that are most needed for assembly. These prioritisations are then used by the gathering algorithm to decide which base item to gather. An important point is that the taken decisions are exchanged amongst the agents to avoid conflicts and unwanted parallel work.

One advantage of the stockpiling strategy is that it creates job idle time, respectively agents available for dismantling, building, and exploration because not all agents are always striving for fulfilling the currently available jobs. Particularly, this additional freedom for individual context-specific decisions of the agents is fostering the adaptation and reaction to varying opponent strategies.

The exploration of the environment is implemented with the so_data library of RHBP in a decentralised and self-organised manner. The framework extension of RHBP containing so_data has been introduced in [9] and enables implicit coordination through various self-organisation patterns. Self-organisation patterns are reusable design patterns abstracted from specific self-organisation algorithms, respectively self-organisation mechanisms [3]. The patterns are classified in movement patterns, decision patterns, and basic functionality patterns.

Basic Functionality Patterns are represented by gradients. Gradients are subject to spreading, aggregation and evaporation. The exchanged gradient messages (*SoMessages*) contain the position where they were emitted, as well as other information and metadata, necessary for advanced patterns to base their calculations on. Movement Patterns are used to control movement of the agents to allow for implementation of behaviours like foraging, chemotaxis, and exploration. Decision patterns allow agents to make collective decisions. The framework provides samples of these behaviours including Quorum Sensing, Morphogenesis and Gossip.

In our MAPC implementation, each agent emits its own location with *SoMessages*, so others do not explore these points as well, while selecting a target location close-by that has not been visited for the longest time. The exchanged SoMessages are filtered in a decentralised manner in each agent by the SoBuffer module instance of the so_data library, which provides the base for the calculation of a discrete heat map. Likewise, the heat map is used to select the appropriate exploration target locations, while the initial exploration phase is stopped after resource nodes for all available base items have been discovered. Later during the match, one drone agent is also exclusively patrolling the map border to discover opponent wells, which would be difficult to discover accidentally during normal job operation.

The general idea behind the well-building is to build wells at locations that are difficult to discover or difficult to reach by the agents of the other team to neglect the requirement of an explicit well defence strategy. The introduction of well building in MAPC 2018 further emphasised the role differences between the agents. Particularly, some locations are only reachable by drones (e.g. some parks, rivers) because there are no close-by roads to allow other agent roles approaching these locations. These locations make great spots for wells as only drones can reach them, so the opponent would need to use drones for dismantling. This strategy has the advantage that not all opponent agents are able to attack our wells as well as that drones in general are very inefficient for dismantling purposes, although this is at the same time a trade-off for the well building because our drones are also inefficient in building up wells. Nevertheless, the strategy has the potential to confuse the opponent because it either needs special consideration or advanced adaptation capabilities.

Dismantling opponent wells keeps the opponent from gaining score points and it allows to gain additional money for further construction of one's own wells.

After an opposing well is discovered, the dismantling behaviour is executed by all agents that are not busy building wells themselves. In particular the agents are prioritising the closest near-by wells for dismantling. The dismantling itself is not further coordinated amongst the agents thus combined or split attacks by groups of agents emerge from the situation.

4   Architecture

The agent architecture of TUBDAI is based on the 2017 approach but replaces big parts of the ROS-topic-based communication in the perception with custom information provider modules, which are feeding the information more directly into RHBP sensors. The information providers avoid some communication overhead coming from ROS communication to increase the efficiency of the implementation. Furthermore, the TUBDAI implementation shares information distributively with the self-organisation library so_data of RHBP.

Figure 1 shows the general architecture as well as how the individual components communicate. The MASSim contest server is running the actual contest simulation and sending the percepts to all agents as well as receiving chosen actions using an XML-based protocol. Each *mac_ros_bridge* receives percepts for one agent, converts them into ROS messages and publishes them into the ROS runtime environment, respectively communication space. Additionally, the bridge takes action messages from the agent and converts them back into an XML format to be passed to the contest server. Each agent in the simulation requires a dedicated *mac_ros_bridge* and one *RHBP Agent*. *RHBP Agent* is a ROS node and is responsible for receiving environment information from the *mac_ros_bridge*, deciding for the best action and communicating the decision to the bridge. Hence, a *RHBP Agent* follows the sense-think-act paradigm within the ROS runtime environment. Each *RHBP Agent* consists of several components, including RHBP components like Behaviours, Sensors, Effects, Conditions and Goals. Additionally, we make use of the *DecisionPattern* from the self-organisation extensions. Particularly, we also use the pattern not only in the way the framework intended it but extensively for all kinds of decisions that do not necessarily involve self-organisation. Basically, this pattern allows to easily share further calculated sensor information between behaviour objects and decision objects. Thus, a certain calculation can be used twice, first, for the task-level decision with RHBP, secondly, for the particular implementation of a behaviour. The design pattern that was used to implement *DecisionPattern* was found to be very useful in many situations and therefore was reused for other components. The *DecisionPattern* is not visualised in the architecture diagram, it is used within the particular behaviour implementations or condition objects.

Providers are responsible for most interaction between *RHBP Agent* and other components like *mac_ros_bridge* and the graphhopper node. They subscribe to messages from the *mac_ros_bridge*, pre-process them and keep them ready for various components to use. This reduces the number of subscribers, and also improves performance by eliminating duplicate code execution that would be necessary if each component would subscribe individually. Providers can also send actions to the *mac_ros_bridge* and interact with the graphhopper node.

The GraphHopper node is responsible for calculating distances between given locations. This allows other components to estimate the steps required to achieve their goals.

The manager component of RHBP retrieves the status of all RHBP components and is responsible for the task-level decision-making that leads to the execution of a behaviour at the end. The chosen behaviour then emits an action through the Action Provider to the *mac_ros_bridge*, which sends it to the MAS-Sim server.

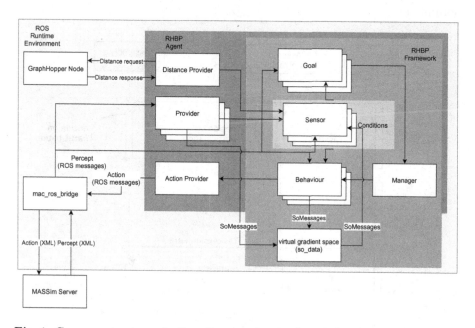

Fig. 1. Component communication diagram showing how information flows between components. The architecture is simplified to only show components that interact with others.

5 Coordination

In this section we are providing more details about our different approaches for coordination within our implementation. First, we explain the explicit coordination with a contract net that is used to coordinate the job fulfilment. Secondly, we discuss details of the implicit coordination for the self-organised exploration and information gathering about opponent well locations.

5.1 Contract Net

A Contract Net with Confirmation Protocol (CNCP) [18] is used to coordinate assembly and job coordination explicitly. This light-weight flexible and fast protocol provides scalability, robustness against errors, adaptivity and few communication bottlenecks [13]. For both of these tasks, one agent initiates the coordination by starting an auction, not to be confused by the auction jobs of the simulation, and requests help from other agents. Next, other agents that are able to help send bids. Our implementation is limited to one coordination taking place at a time. If another agent has already initiated coordination, the agent has to wait until the current coordination cycle is complete before starting its coordination.

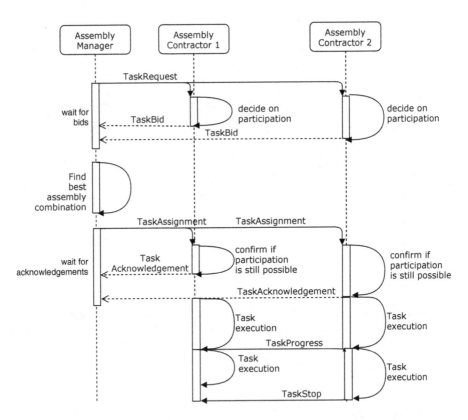

Fig. 2. Interaction diagram of assembly with one initiating manager and two participating contractors.

When an agent has filled up its stock, it initiates the assembly process by starting the assembly manager (see Fig. 2). The manager requests all other agents to send bids to help with assembly. If another agent wants to coordinate, it first has to wait until the current coordination cycle is finished. Other agents then respond with their bid which includes their location, role, and the items they can offer. Once the manager decides for a combination, it sends assignments to all chosen agents. The agents then return an acknowledgement and the assembly can start. Participating agents coordinate assembly by sending a *TaskProgress* message. At any time, agents can interrupt assembly by sending a *StopTask* message, which forces all participating agents to stop their task. This could happen, when one agent receives a job task, which has a higher priority than assembly tasks.

The job coordination strategy works similar to assembly coordination strategy. It is initiated when a job component decides for a job to execute. The JobManager then sends out an initial request. Each agent that doesn't have an active task checks if they can help with the task and respond with the items they can offer. The manager then looks for a combination of agents that can perform the job and sends out an assignment to all of them. The agents confirm by sending an acknowledgement back and the task is started. Similar to the assembly CNP, the task can be stopped at any time by emitting the *StopTask* message.

5.2 Self-organisation

The self-organisation extension for RHBP allows agents to share information about their environment in a virtual gradient space, which can then be used for implicit coordination [9].

In our implementation agents publish self-organisation messages whenever they move around to let all other agents know which parts of the map they have visited. The receiving agents then aggregate these messages from all agents in a distributed fashion. This allows them to decide which locations require further exploration, which is especially relevant in the initial exploration phase to detect all necessary resource nodes in the beginning of each simulation. This self-organisation exploration algorithm is enhanced further by using two other types of messages. Agents publish the location they plan to go to, so other agents are able to avoid it. This allows for the prevention of exploring certain locations twice at the same time. Moreover, agents publish a message when a location is not reachable, so other agents do not try to go there.

In detail, we are creating a heat map from self-organisation messages of specific frames, indicating either how often each spot has been subject to said frames or the last *SoMessage* that has been recorded at each position. The heat map is realised using a grid of numbers instead of a vector-based system. This reduces the accuracy but greatly simplifies later calculations. Initially, the decision pattern creates a two-dimensional array filled with zeros, which represents the map. Whenever a *SoMessage* arrives, that matches one of the desired frames, the map is updated. The location of the *SoMessage* is converted to a mask. The mask is then applied to the map. *MapDecision* has two modes, *oldest_visited* and *seen_count* Depending on the mode, the mask is applied to the existing map to result in a heat map indicating how often a location has been visited, or when each location has been visited last.

The other way self-organisation is used for coordination is for agents to check if an opponent well has successfully been dismantled. Whenever an agent locates an opponent's well, it informs all other agents about it through SoMessages. Agents combine this information with location information sent by other agents. If at some point, the well is not seen anymore, even when an agent is in range of the well, the agent can be sure, that the well has been successfully dismantled.

6 RHBP Behaviour Model

A RHBP behaviour model allows to describe the relationships between behaviours, goals, and sensors through conditions and effects. These models provide the foundation for the autonomous decision-making executed in the manager component of RHBP.

In contrast to the last-years participation of TUB using RHBP with a single behaviour model layer for decision-making, our implementation partitions the model into various nested behaviour models. This became possible through the recently introduced NetworkBehaviour feature. NetworkBehaviours are frequently used for structuring and controlling the major responsibilities of the agents on the highest decision-making level. Such partitioning fosters a separation of concerns, reuse of code, and a reduction of the decision-space through grouping of certain behaviour options. NetworkBehaviours are a special type of behaviours that directly inherit from the behaviour base class of RHBP. In contrast to normal behaviour implementations in RHBP, the NetworkBehaviours are not directly executing any actions that have an influence on the environment. Instead, NetworkBehaviours are triggering a nested decision-making and planning process to select suitable behaviours from their encapsulated behaviour model to achieve the targeted effects.

In particular, NetworkBehaviours are modelled for controlling resource exploration, discovering opponent wells, dismantling opponent wells, building wells, gathering base items, assembling finished item products, and delivering jobs. All NetworkBehaviour implementations are inheriting from an abstract scenario-specific NetworkBehaviour implementation GoAndDoNetworkBehaviour that incorporates battery management and travelling on the simulated map, which is a basic capability of all higher-level tasks in the MAPC scenario. The high-level decision-making behaviour model is visualised in Fig. 3. It shows the high-level first class entities and their relationships, this in turn describes the agent behaviour declaratively. Here, it has to mentioned that all further implicit dependencies are automatically determined by the system. Hence, there is no direct relationship between behaviours and goals in the shown model.

Considering the fact that this model covers only the highest-level of decision-making with additional nested models within each of the shown NetworkBehaviours a comparison with the model of the previous participation in 2017, please see [10], indicates that the complexity of the 2018 TUBDAI implementation is considerably larger. Overall, we see that the structure of TUBDAI is more fine-grained, e.g. we have distinct NetworkBehaviours for assembly, delivery, and gathering. Likewise, the entire number of behaviour and goal instances is considerably larger but this is partly because of redundant charging goals and behaviours in each NetworkBehaviour. In detail, the old TUBDAI model contained only 5 behaviours and 2 goals, whereas TUBDAI 2018 has 3 goals and 7 NetworkBehaviours each again containing 2 goals and 4–5 behaviours.

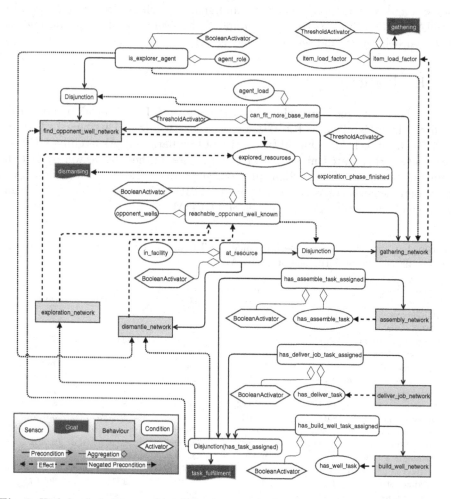

Fig. 3. High-level decision-making behaviour model for agent task execution of TUB-DAI 2018. All listed behaviours are NetworkBehaviours containing nested behaviour models. Each NetworkBehaviour contains 2 goals and 4–5 behaviours.

During the realisation of the TUBDAI implementation we discovered a new general implementation pattern for lower-level decisions in sensor, condition, behaviour, and goal implementations. The new implementation pattern is taken from the self-organisation extension of RHBP, which offers a component called DecisionPattern that can be used by certain behaviours and sensors to share low-level decisions between the decision-making layer of RHBP and the actual implementation of the behaviour. This implementation pattern is further generalised and not anymore applied only for self-organisation related low-level decisions. Instead, the DecisionPattern works as an aggregate that takes a low-level decision like selecting the closest charging station, which is then shared amongst the sensors and conditions of behaviours and goals as well as the actual behaviour implementation. This pattern was found to be useful for sharing information between behaviours and sensors of one agent.

7   Evaluation

Four other teams participated in the 2018 contest: SMART_JaCaMo (Pontifícia Universidade Católica do Rio Grande do Sul (PUCRS)), Dumping to Gather (TUB), Jason-DTU (Technical University of Denmark) and Akuanduba-UDESC (Santa Catarina State University (UDESC)). Three of these teams were defeated, only one team was able to win against our submission. Table 1 shows main stats that were achieved by each team against TUBDAI. The last column shows an average of these stats for all matches of TUBDAI.

Table 1. Comparison of the performance of all teams in the matches with TUBDAI vs overall average performance of TUBDAI.

Team	Jason-DTU	Akuanduba-UDESC	Dumping to Gather	SMART_-JaCaMo	TUBDAI (avg)
Ranking	3	5	4	1	2
Match points	0	0	0	9	6.75
Tournament points	21	0	9	33	27
Successful jobs	83	0	35	163	79
Opponent jobs	71	127	94	24	70.25
Score after 3 matches	2236	0	2206	2923	45628.75
Opponent score	57619	71928	42935	10033	1841
No actions	15.92%	97.95%	10.40%	8.33%	8.88%
Opponent no action	8.07%	2.51%	6.40%	18.53%	33.15%
Goto actions	58695	993	70730	73039	75648.25
Goto failure rate	30.92%	41.29%	43.27%	0.00%	0.70%
Dismantle actions	0	0	3354	1780	1471
Retrieve & delivered	1078	0	94	2000	0
Build actions	402	0	1336	1371	3604.75
Successful assembly	712	688	293	1350	378
Agent upgrades	0	0	0	14	0

In the following subsections we will briefly summarise the most important observations we made during the matches against each opponent, before we finally discuss our performance and results in more detail. If the reader wants to replicate our observations the source code of all teams, the simulation server, and replays from all matches are available on the official contest homepage[1].

---

[1] https://multiagentcontest.org/2018/.

7.1   Jason-DTU

Jason-DTU won the second place in the previous edition of the contest and also exhibited a good performing and successful solution in this year's contest.

To finish jobs, Jason-DTU makes excessive use of storages and specialised task groups. Particularly, they use certain road agents for item gathering as well as specialised agent teams for taking care of assembly and delivery. When there is enough massium available, trucks move to the edge of the map and build wells there.

While the team had an aggressive dismantling strategy against other teams, during the match against TUBDAI, the team did not perform any dismantle action. As shown in Table 1, the team had a 30.92% failure rate of the goto action. This likely results from road agents trying to dismantle wells, but not being able to reach them as they were built at off-road locations.

Their job strategy was very effective, due to the centralised workshop and storage being used as intermediary item holder reduced the coordination efforts. As items are stockpiled, the jobs can be performed quickly while also keeping the agent's efficiency on a high level. This led to a slightly better job performance of 83 jobs executed, compared to 79 jobs on average in three simulations for TUBDAI.

7.2   Akuanduba-UDESC

The second opponent in the contest was Akuanduba-UDESC. Due to an error in their system, the team could not send actions in time. This resulted in almost no actions by their agents.

Due to the inaction of this team's agents, their strategy cannot be analysed. However, it allows to evaluate our submission in a very special case. Due to the fact, that effectively no opponent was present, no dismantling was needed. This allowed the agents to shift more resources to job execution.

While the average job execution rate of our team against all other teams was 63 jobs, during the matches against Akuanduba-UDESC, the job execution rate was 127 job (see Table 1). This shows that our agents adapted well to a situation without opponent wells by shifting priorities accordingly.

7.3   Dumping to Gather

Dumping to Gather, the other team from TUB, started with the same basis for their project including the mac_ros_bridge and RHBP as framework. However, they followed the different on-demand strategy for job execution. When a job was announced, they coordinated agent teams who were then responsible for the whole chain of actions including gathering, assembly and delivery.

Their approach to build wells was to use multiple agents of all roles at the same time. This allowed them to build up wells almost instantly but had the drawback of multiple agents having to use many steps for moving to the desti-nation location. Wells were built next to each other in a line. We assume this was done to reduce the number of movement steps that had to be taken between building two wells. However, this has the disadvantage that dismantling agents usually immediately after dismantling one well find the next one. This allowed our team to dismantle their wells relatively quickly.

Dismantling was done using both air and road agents. This allowed Dumping to Gather to attack our wells that were placed in off-road locations using drones. However, other agents were not prepared to handle off-road locations and got stuck in an error loop, trying to reach the wells. This led to a goto action failure rate of 43.27% (see Table 1).

7.4   SMART_JaCaMo

The team SMART_JaCaMo was a very strong opponent in multiple regards. First, the team's agents seem to have been divided into different responsibilities, six trucks were used to only build wells, two drones were only used for exploration and dismantling and the rest performing jobs.

Secondly, the team was able to perform 163 jobs, which was substantially more than any other team (see Table 1). The agents who were tasked with job execution, gathered items, assembled them together and delivered them according to the available jobs. They also made use of storing items in storages in order to improve efficiency.

Thirdly, when enough massium was available, a number of truck-agents were responsible for building wells. The locations seemed to have been chosen randomly somewhere close to the edge of the map.

Finally, dismantling was done by two drones. Their skill was upgraded at simulation start, so they can perform dismantling actions efficiently. Afterwards they were only responsible for finding wells and dismantling them. As drones are able to go to off-road locations, this defeated our strategy pretty well. Due to the road-agents not dismantling at all, they also did not suffer from failed goto actions like other teams.

7.5   Discussion

All in all, the last-minute changes of the well-building strategy paid off because this has been a unique strategy, which was not expected by the opponents. Here, this particular strategy becomes especially attractive, as the original well-building strategy has been changed three days before the contest and the RHBP-based architecture supported a quick integration of the new strategy, which did not require comprehensive code changes. Originally, it was the plan to build wells with trucks at the edges of the map area. Unfortunately, this turned out to be less efficient with the final contest maps published three days before the contest. Instead, we shifted to the strategy that making use of so-called off-road locations on the map in order to neglect an explicit well defence strategy. Off-road locations are locations that are not connected to the street network and thus only reachable by drones.

The conducted last-minute changes comprise shifted role responsibilities like only drones building wells; a changed exploration that is not focusing anymore on the map borders; less priority on the job fulfilment because the mandatory and rare drones are often busy with well-building; and a higher priority on dismantling to efficiently use the increased job idle time for non-drone agents.

The encapsulation of code within behaviours and aggregation in NetworkBehaviours made these changes very intuitive and robust. By duplicating certain NetworkBehaviours and switching around preconditions and effects, most of the strategy was adapted, requiring only small code changes within the behaviours. In our opinion this would have been potentially much more difficult to achieve with a traditional sequential programming approach.

The runtime adaptiveness of RHBP could be observed at the match against Akuanduba-UDESC. While many resources were usually used for dismantling opponent wells, there was no dismantling required against Akuanduba-UDESC because of their timeout issues, which resulted in almost 100% inactivity of their agents. This freed up resources for other tasks for our agents. The agents were able to adapt to this unexpected situation and increased their job performance from an average of 63 jobs to 127 jobs. This shows that TUBDAI agents adapted well to a situation without opponent wells by shifting priorities accordingly.

Moreover, the simulation configuration used in the contest was very different from the sample configurations that have been published together with the server source code for the contest preparation. The biggest difference was that it was very easy to gain money for building wells within the contest. While in the sample configurations (which we assumed to be similar to the contest configuration) most jobs offered rewards of less than 500, the jobs in the contest had much higher rewards, , i.e. jobs exceeding 10,000 in reward, whereas building wells stayed on the same price level. In consequence, building wells became easier, and the strategy of building and defending more critical. Nevertheless, the TUBDAI implementation has shown that it was able to adapt and handle this unexpected setup successfully.

In the end, *TUBDAI* only lost the final match against SMART_JaCaMo. The reason was that they efficiently dismantled our non-defended off-road constructed wells exclusively with two of their drones, which have been only responsible for discovering and dismantling of our wells. Moreover, their skill was upgraded directly at simulation start, so they dismantled more efficiently. Furthermore, due to the road-agents not dismantling at all, team SMART_JaCaMo did not suffer from failed goto actions like other teams. A question that might come up at this point is why our RHBP-based approach was not able to adapt automatically to this situation. The reason is that RHBP is only having the opportunity of adaptation if alternative behaviour implementations are available, which was not the case for the TUBDAI implementation.

Nevertheless, a detailed analysis of the replays and the published code of SMART_JaCaMo showed that their unique strategy was also not a result of their adaptive strategy or implementation, but rather a result of their last-minute changes in implementation the human team has made after analysing the matches before the very last match of the competition between TUBDAI and SMART_JaCaMo. We could prove this by playing about 30 simulations with the a priori published simulation sample configurations and the not modified SMART_JaCaMo code in which SMART_JaCaMo was not able to win any simulation against our team. In detail, the SMART_JaCaMo team added a second drone for exploration, implemented immediate skill upgrade after simulation start, disabled dismantling in trucks, enabled dismantling for exploration drones, and created a second drone exploration algorithm, that targets locations that are typically used by our agents to build wells. All these changes were made in short time-frame while we were competing against the other three teams. The changes seemed to be very robust and side-effect free, which is impressive for such a substantial last-minute change. Nevertheless, it has to be stated that the SMART_JaCaMo approach did not follow the rules of the competition because teams are encouraged to refrain from code changes during the contest that are not pure bug fixes of their own strategy. This fact also leads to an official correction of the final placement by the steering committee of the competition resulting in a shared top spot between TUBDAI and team SMART_JaCaMo[2].

8   Conclusion

In the presented article we described our successful solution for the MAPC 2018 that allowed us to win the shared top spot of the competition. Our solution enabled us to address the described challenges of the contest. The required coordination is achieved by a combination of explicit coordination based on a contract net protocol, and implicit coordination on the foundation of the RHBP self-organisation extension. Here, both coordination approaches are also supporting a decentralised solution. Adapting to varying environments and situations was possible through the application of our framework RHBP that fosters a separation of concerns of agent capabilities, which are then used for autonomous decision-making. Moreover, this autonomous decision-making enabled our system to quickly react on different opponent behaviours. The given computational constraints and requirement to handle an increased number of agents in comparison to the previous year have also been addressed successfully.

All in all, we could show that a multi-agent system developed on the foundation of our RHBP framework is able to compete with other multi-agent approaches even though it is actually targeting the different application domain of multi-robot system. Particularly, using RHBP showed to be advantageous especially in terms of adaptation capabilities during development as well as in runtime of the system. Furthermore, our focus in 2018 on testing in practise the recently introduced RHBP features for creating behaviour model hierarchies by nesting and encapsulating behaviours and goals within other behaviours as well as realising implicit coordination through sharing and filtering information with the support of our self-organisation extension turned out to be beneficial.

---

[2] https://multiagentcontest.org/2019/01/23/results.html.

For the future, we would like to further explore the challenge of selecting the most appropriate high-level strategy like on-demand job completion or stockpiling in such a complex scenario. So far the high-level strategy, even though successful in our case, is the result of human considerations and engineering. Future work could explore if we are able to select autonomously the most appropriate high-level strategy, especially by applying RHBP, from several implemented strategies depending on the opponent's behaviour.

1   Team Overview: Short Answers

1.1   Participants and Their Background

What was your motivation to participate in the contest?
The motivation was to further evaluate the decision-making and planning framework ROS Hybrid Behaviour Planner (RHBP). While the framework has been used in a wide variety of projects (also in MAPC 2017), newer features have not been tested in complex scenarios. One of those features allows to create multiple independent levels of decision making by encapsulating a separate behaviour network into a behaviour. Another one is an extension for implicit coordination on the foundation of self-organisation.

What is the history of your group? (course project, thesis, ...)
Researchers of the DAI-Labor started to participate in the contest in 2007. Since then they have contributed to every edition of the contest and have won four of them using successive generations of the JIAC multi-agent framework. The TUBDAI 2018 team originates from a Master's Thesis student and its supervising PhD student. The applied framework RHBP is developed in one Ph.D. thesis and several independent Bachelor and Master's theses.

What is your field of research? Which work therein is related?
Our field of research is multi-agent systems applied in the robotics domain.

1.2   Development

How much time did you invest in the contest for
programming vs. other tasks (for example organization)?
creating vs. optimizing your agents?
We invested approximately 600 h without time for framework development and the communication proxy (mac_ros_bridge). The mac_ros_bridge maps the xml-based socket communication of the MASSim simulation server to ROS communication means (which was also partly reused from MAPC 2017). Furthermore, 400 h of the invested time budget are spend on programming tasks while 200 h are used for optimising our approach.

How many lines of code did you produce for your final agent team?
The scenario specific code contains approximately 7000 LOC.

How many people were involved and to which degree?

Christopher-Eyk Hrabia (Ph.D. Student at Technische Universität Berlin) provided the general supervision, was especially responsible for the consultation about scientific approaches as well as giving technical support for the RHBP framework and its application.

Michael Franz Ettlinger (M.Sc. Student at Technische Universität Berlin) was responsible for the scenario specific implementation and execution of the contest.

Axel Hessler (Post-Doc at Technische Universität Berlin) was responsible for the infrastructure and overall administration.

When did you start working on your agents?

The major work started mid May 2018, communication infrastructure (e.g. mac_ros_bridge) was already done mid of April 2018.

1.3 System Details

How do your agents work together? (coordination, information sharing, ...)

Information sharing for implicit coordination (exploration, opponent well states) as well as explicit coordination (jobs) through a contract-net protocol implementation.

What are critical components of your team?

The most critical component is the job planning component which coordinates the job tasks amongst the agents.

Can your agents change their behaviour during runtime? If so, what triggers the changes?

Yes. The agents select the most appropriate behaviour based on the current perception and the results of the hybrid planning decision-making component of RHBP.

Did you have to make changes to the team (e.g. fix critical bugs) during the contest?

No.

How do you organize your agents? Do you use e.g. hierarchies? Is your organization implicit or explicit?

No hierarchy. We partly use implicit (self-organised) and partly explicit (contract-net protocol) coordination, see above.

Is most of your agents' behaviour emergent on an individual or team level?

All behaviour if it was possible emerge from individual level, which results from the autonomously taken decision by each individual agent.

If your agents perform some planning, how many steps do they plan ahead?

They plan one task ahead. A task can technically have unlimited amount of steps but practically has no more than 40 simulation steps.

If you have a perceive-think-act cycle, how is it synchronized with the server?

Our perceive-think-act cycle is performed as quick as possible as soon as the server delivers the percept of the current simulation step. Through enough calculation power it was made sure that the actions are always delivered in time.

How did you go about debugging your system?

We applied three different debugging techniques. First, RHBP offers extensions visualisation and monitoring of behaviours and their internal states. Secondly, agents can be started in development environment and analysed with a normal Python debugger. Thirdly, we used custom log messages to analyse the runtime behaviour without interference.

Which operating system did you use, and is your team portable to other operating systems?

We used Ubuntu 16.04, our solution is portable to all other Linux distributions that have ROS support. Execution on Windows is also possible through the Windows Subsystem for Linux (WSL) using a Ubuntu-binding.

What hardware did you use to run your agent team? (RAM, CPU, disk space, multiple computers, any other notable requirements)

Intel(R) Core(TM) i7-4930K @ 3.40 GHz CPU (6 cores with hyper-threading), 32 GB RAM and a Samsung SSD 840. It is the same machine that was used already by our team in MAPC 2017.

1.4   Scenario and Strategy

What is the main strategy of your agent team?

Our strategy has three main tiers. Stockpiling items as well as assembled items. Building wells at positions that are only accessible for special agents (drones). Attacking opponent wells aggressively.

How do your agents decide which jobs to complete?

If all required items are on stock the jobs are completed.

Do you have different strategies for the different roles?

Yes, only drones build wells and one drone is responsible for well exploration at the map border.

Do your agents form ad-hoc teams to complete a task?

Yes, the sub-tasks of a job are coordinated ad-hoc with a contract-net protocol implementation. Here, all agents participate in the auctions that are used for the task assignment.

How do your agents decide when and where to build wells?

Random places that can't be reached by other agents (off-road). We use the Graphhopper back-end to determine which map locations are not accessible by road agents.

If your agents accumulated a lot of currency, why did they not spend it immediately?

Our strategy requires drones to execute the well building, due to the fact that drones are comparable inefficient in building it is possible that we accumulate currency if the drones are not able to build fast enough.

1.5   And the Moral of It Is ...

What did you learn from participating in the contest?
What are the strong and weak points of your team?

The strategy decisions proved to be a viable solution for the contest. The stockpile with feedback strategy worked good enough to produce the required money (massium) for wells, while providing enough idle agent time for other tasks. If the contest would have been about massium alone (like last year) the strategy in its current implementation would likely preform worse. In such a scenario the use of storages could massively improve the massium output but would reduce the availability of agents for well building tasks. The off-road well locations strategy was not expected by any opponent and therefore performed well. The main drawback of the strategy was that if it is expected, it is easy to counter. This was observable in the match against SMART JaCaMo, who were able to adapt their strategy in a few hours to beat our team. The only assumption that turned out wrong was that we expected opponents to try to defend their wells once they were built. RHBP proved to be a great framework to use for the project. After an initial learning period, RHBP bore out to be robust and allowed agents to adapt well to changes at run time. The implementation was robust and performed well during the contest. The assembly coordination strategy worked well but resulted in many empty coordination cycles. If this would have been implemented using a client initiating contract net protocol, its performance as well as simplicity would likely have increased.

How viable were your chosen programming language, methodology, tools, and algorithms?

One goal of this project was to use RHBP and its new features and extensions, evaluate them and offer improvement suggestions. RHBP was used quite successfully and allowed to create a fast, adaptive and flexible solution for the contest. It also allowed quick and robust changes to the strategy as discussed in the evaluation. The run-time adaptiveness of RHBP could be observed at the match against Akuanduba-UDESC. While many resources were usually used for dismantling opponent wells, there was no dismantling required against Akuanduba-UDESC, which freed up resources for other tasks.

Did you encounter new problems during the contest?

We have been able to find several bugs and performance bottle necks in our SoBuffer library, which is used for communicating and handling messages for self-organisation.

Did playing against other agent teams bring about new insights on your own agents?

We did not gain major insights, we could only prove the runtime adaptation capabilities in situations we have not especially considered before.

What would you improve if you wanted to participate in the same contest a week from now (or next year)?

We would less emphasis on job completion and would add a well defence strategy.

Which aspect of your team cost you the most time?
Implementing the job coordination and execution.

Why did your team perform as it did? Why did the other teams perform better/worse than you did?
Because other teams didn't expect off-road well locations and our solution adapted robustly to different situations in the games.

1.6   The Future of the MAPC

What can be improved regarding the contest for next year?
Due to incidents in this years contest, we propose to make handing in code before contest obligatory. Furthermore, we think code changes should not be allowed, which also solves the problem of fair schedules. Maybe it could also be a good approach to run everything on the same virtual machines or docker containers, which are running in the organisers department to avoid problems with connection performance or too much deviating hardware requirements. Furthermore, we encourage to focus more on decentralisation and autonomous agent development. while avoiding the focus on optimisation problems.

What kind of scenario would you like to play next? What kind of features should the new scenario have? We would suggest to have a scenario that requires less optimisation of a scenario specific problem, highlighting more features of intelligent agents such as being adaptive, able to learn, robust, ...

Should the teams be allowed to make changes to their agents during the contest (even based on opponent agent behaviour observed in earlier matches)? If yes, should only some changes be legal and which ones (e.g. bugfixes), and how to decide a change's classification? If no, should we ensure that no changes are made and how?
Changes should not be allowed because having modifications during the contest defeats the purpose of finding a great strategy as well as autonomous decision making when developers make decisions based on their observations. Even more, we propose to enforce a code submission before the contest starts. Bugfixes could potentially be allowed but would have to go through a peer-reviewed pull request. For organisational reasons the review of the pull request could also be done after the contest.

Do you have ideas to reduce the impact of unforeseen strategies (e.g., playing a second leg after some time)?
As long as the strategies are done on the foundation of the provided API not exploiting bugs everything should be allowed. Even more, unforeseen strategies should be encouraged.

If the organisers want to prevent this (which we don't think they should), they could request a detailed strategy description to make sure they agree that the strategy is "expected" and not "unforeseen".

References

1. Ahlbrecht, T., Dix, J., Fiekas, N.: Multi-agent programming contest 2017. Ann. Math. Artif. Intell. **84**(1), 1–16 (2018)
2. Ahlbrecht, T., Dix, J., Schlesinger, F.: From testing agent systems to a scalable simulation platform. In: Eiter, T., Strass, H., Truszczyński, M., Woltran, S. (eds.) Advances in Knowledge Representation, Logic Programming, and Abstract Argumentation. LNCS (LNAI), vol. 9060, pp. 47–62. Springer, Cham (2015). https://doi.org/10.1007/978-3-319-14726-0_4
3. Fernandez-Marquez, J.L., Serugendo, G.D.M., Montagna, S., Viroli, M., Arcos, J.L.: Description and composition of bio-inspired design patterns: a complete overview. Nat. Comput. **12**(1), 43–67 (2012)
4. Heßler, A., Hirsch, B., Keiser, J.: Collecting gold. JIAC IV agents in multi-agent programming contest. In: Proceedings of the Fifth International Workshop on Programming Multi-Agent Systems, At AAMAS 2007, Honolulu, HI, USA (2007)
5. Heßler, A., Hirsch, B., Küster, T.: Herding cows with JIAC V. Ann. Math. Artif. Intell. 1–15 (2010). https://doi.org/10.1007/s10472-010-9178-x
6. Heßler, A., Konnerth, T., Napierala, P., Wiemann, B.: Multi-agent programming contest 2012: TUB team description. In: Köster, M., Schlesinger, F., Dix, J. (eds.) The Multi-Agent Programming Contest 2012 Edition: Evaluation and Team Descriptions, number IfI-13-01 in IfI Technical Report Series, pp. 86–97. Institut für Informatik, Technische Universität Clausthal (2013)
7. Hoffmann, J.: The metric-FF planning system: Translating "ignoring delete lists" to numeric state variables. J. Artif. Intell. Res. (JAIR) **20**, 291–341 (2003)
8. Hrabia, C.-E., et al.: An autonomous companion UAV for the SpaceBot cup competition 2015. In: Koubaa, A. (ed.) Robot Operating System (ROS). SCI, vol. 707, pp. 345–385. Springer, Cham (2017). https://doi.org/10.1007/978-3-319-54927-9_11
9. Hrabia, C.-E., Kaiser, T.K., Albayrak, S.: Combining self-organisation with decision-making and planning. In: Belardinelli, F., Argente, E. (eds.) EUMAS/AT-2017. LNCS (LNAI), vol. 10767, pp. 385–399. Springer, Cham (2018). https://doi.org/10.1007/978-3-030-01713-2_27
10. Hrabia, C.-E., Lehmann, P.M., Battjbuer, N., Hessler, A., Albayrak, S.: Applying robotic frameworks in a simulated multi-agent contest. Ann. Math. Artif. Intell. **84**, 117–138 (2018)
11. Hrabia, C.-E., Wypler, S., Albayrak, S.: Towards goal-driven behaviour control of multi-robot systems. In: 2017 3rd International Conference on Control, Automation and Robotics (ICCAR), pp. 166–173, April 2017
12. Jennings, N.R., Sycara, K., Wooldridge, M.: A roadmap of agent research and development. Auton. Agents Multi-Agent Syst. **1**(1), 7–38 (1998)
13. Krakowczyk, D., Wolff, J., Ciobanu, A., Meyer, D.J., Hrabia, C.-E.: Developing a distributed drone delivery system with a hybrid behavior planning system. In: Trollmann, F., Turhan, A.-Y. (eds.) KI 2018. LNCS (LNAI), vol. 11117, pp. 107–114. Springer, Cham (2018). https://doi.org/10.1007/978-3-030-00111-7_10
14. Maes, P.: How to do the right thing. Connect. Sci. **1**(3), 291–323 (1989)
15. Mcdermott, D., et al.: PDDL - The Planning Domain Definition Language (1998)
16. Pieper, J.: Multi-agent programming contest 2017: BusyBeaver team description. Ann. Math. Artif. Intell. **84**, 1–17 (2018)
17. Quigley, M., et al.: ROS: an open-source robot operating system. In: ICRA Workshop on Open Source Software, vol. 3, no. 3.2, p. 5 (2009)

18. Schillo, M., Kray, C., Fischer, K.: The eager bidder problem: a fundamental problem of DAI and selected solutions. In: Proceedings of the first International Joint Conference on Autonomous Agents and Multiagent Systems: Part 2, pp. 599–606. ACM (2002)
19. Smith, R.G.: The contract net protocol: high-level communication and control in a distributed problem solver. IEEE Trans. Comput. **12**, 1104–1113 (1980)

Correction to: The Multi-Agent Programming Contest 2018 - A Third Time in the City

Tobias Ahlbrecht ⓘ, Jürgen Dix ⓘ, and Niklas Fiekas ⓘ

Correction to:
**Chapter "The Multi-Agent Programming Contest 2018 -
A Third Time in the City" in: T. Ahlbrecht et al. (Eds.):**
The Multi-Agent Programming Contest 2018, **LNAI 11957,**
https://doi.org/10.1007/978-3-030-37959-9_1

In the original version of chapter 1 the authors stated that TUBDAI's opponents did not "think of" TUBDAI's strategy, which they now think was a poor choice of words to relay the message. The text has now been updated to clarify that some teams were aware of this strategy but did not expect it to be used.

The updated version of this chapter can be found at
https://doi.org/10.1007/978-3-030-37959-9_1

© Springer Nature Switzerland AG 2020
T. Ahlbrecht et al. (Eds.): MAPC 2018, LNAI 11957, p. C1, 2020.
https://doi.org/10.1007/978-3-030-37959-9_7

Author Index

Printed in the United States
By Bookmasters